DIALOGUING ACROSS CULTURES, IDENTITIES, AND LEARNING

Drawing on dialogical self theory, this book presents a new framework for social and cultural identity construction in the literacy classroom, offering possibilities for how teachers might adjust their pedagogy to better support the range of cultural stances present in all classrooms.

In the complex multicultural/multiethnic/multilingual contexts of learning in and out of school spaces today, students and teachers are constantly dialoguing across cultures, both internally and externally, and these cultures are in dialogue with each other. The authors unpack some of the complexity of culture and identity, what people do with culture and identity, and how people navigate multiple cultures and identities. Readers are invited to re-examine how they view different cultures and the roles these play in their lives, and to dialogue with the authors about cultures, learning, literacy, identity, and agency.

Bob Fecho is Professor of English Education, Teachers College, Columbia University, USA.

Jennifer Clifton is Assistant Professor, Department of English (Rhetoric and Writing Studies), The University of Texas at El Paso, USA.

LANGUAGE, CULTURE, AND TEACHING
SONIA NIETO, SERIES EDITOR

Visit www.routledge.com/education for additional information on titles in the
Language, Culture, and Teaching series.

DIALOGUING ACROSS CULTURES, IDENTITIES, AND LEARNING

Crosscurrents and Complexities in Literacy Classrooms

Bob Fecho
Jennifer Clifton

Routledge
Taylor & Francis Group

NEW YORK AND LONDON

First published 2017
by Routledge
711 Third Avenue, New York, NY 10017

and by Routledge
2 Park Square, Milton Park, Abingdon, Oxon, OX14 4RN

Routledge is an imprint of the Taylor & Francis Group, an informa business

© 2017 Taylor & Francis

The right of Bob Fecho and Jennifer Clifton to be identified as authors of this work has been asserted by them in accordance with sections 77 and 78 of the Copyright, Designs and Patents Act 1988.

Trademark notice: Product or corporate names may be trademarks or registered trademarks, and are used only for identification and explanation without intent to infringe.

Library of Congress Cataloging in Publication Data
Names: Fecho, Bob, author. | Clifton, Jennifer, author.
Title: Dialoguing across cultures, identities, and learning : crosscurrents and complexities in literacy classrooms / by Bob Fecho, Jennifer Clifton.
Description: New York, NY : Routledge, 2016. | Includes bibliographical references and index.
Identifiers: LCCN 2016012578| ISBN 9781138998582 (hardback) | ISBN 9781138998599 (pbk.) | ISBN 9781315658629 (ebook)
Subjects: LCSH: Literacy–Social aspects. | Language arts–Social aspects. | Interaction analysis in education. | Multicultural education.
Classification: LCC LC149 .F44 2016 | DDC 302.2244–dc23
LC record available at https://lccn.loc.gov/2016012578

ISBN: 978-1-138-99858-2 (hbk)
ISBN: 978-1-138-99859-9 (pbk)
ISBN: 978-1-315-65862-9 (ebk)

Typeset in Bembo
by Cenveo Publisher Services

This book is dedicated to the Raymonds, Isaacs, Cassies, and Ians who continue to teach us and amaze us, and to the hard and hopeful work of making sites of learning interesting, joyful, and just places for us all.

CONTENTS

ACKNOWLEDGEMENTS

We both would like to thank Sonia Nieto for first approaching Bob with an invitation to write for this series, for showing great patience as he dragged his feet while trying to think of a suitable project, and for being the inspiration to all of us in multicultural education. Naomi Silverman, our editor at Routledge, not only believed in this book from the start, but right from the get go told us so enthusiastically. Also, we're indebted to Brianna Pennella, Kristin Susser, and Hélène Feest—all part of the production team at Taylor & Francis—who shepherded this book through the process. We would be remiss for not thanking Jim Baumann and Lenny Sanchez for first introducing Jen to Bob's work and suggesting that we might like to know each other.

In addition, Jen would like to thank Bob for inviting her to be part of this project and for being wonderfully open to the directions she wanted to pursue. Anything Jen writes is always already in dialogue with her partner and favorite Pirate-Ruffian-Gypsy whose prodigal love is both anchor and inspiration.

And Bob would like to thank his partner Janette who never fails to make him feel that he can do just about anything he sets his mind to, and Alice the cat, his constant New York apartment companion.

INTRODUCTION

Consider a scenario in which a young man is in a classroom where he is the only Black person. In such an instance, race may feel uppermost to that young man in terms of representation, but being male, an adolescent, a Baptist, gay, a video game player, a Photoshop expert, a baseball player, and a lover of classical music still figures in the ongoing interaction. Some kid, eh? He, along with the rest of the class, is reading Bill Konigsberg's *Out of the Pocket*, a young adult novel in which a White all-star quarterback is outed by a student journalist just as he is being recruited by top college teams. As he reads this book in a small southern town near a large army base, he starts to consider his response to the text.

How might this young Black man reading this novel respond internally to the novel, to his classmates, to his life as a whole? In a class discussion and in other situations in his life, how might he respond? As a Baptist? As a Gay Youth? As a young Black Man? Would he take up some intersection of these cultural identities; for example, would he respond as a *Black* Gay Baptist Man? Or would he elevate and project these differently, foregrounding another identity in this combination; for example, would he respond as a *Gay* Black Baptist Man or a *Baptist* Black Gay Man?

These are not simply questions of semantics. They are questions of cultures and identities in dialogue within a single self, a single body. To be part of a culture is to somehow share in the values and practices that culture counts as membership. And yet a person might self-identify in a particular way—perhaps as being gay—even without a sense of belonging to an LGBTQ culture or without others recognizing or even knowing that he is gay. To self-identify is to recognize a personal sense of self in a particular way—a recognition that may or may not involve certain interests or certain ways of thinking, being, talking that others also share.

But what does a person do when one way of seeing oneself conflicts with another way of seeing oneself, or when the values and practices of one of his cultures conflict with the values and practices of another of their cultures? For example, what does this young man do if the Baptist culture he's part of says that being gay means that he is not Baptist? Or if the particular Black culture he sees himself part of sees being gay as something that undermines his membership with others who are Black, perhaps especially with those who are Black and Baptist? Or if other young men see being gay as something that undercuts who he is as a man, a phenomenon sociologist C.J. Pascoe (2007) has documented well? Or if his being Gay also maintains space for his being Black, Baptist and a Man?

Of course, there are spectrums and intersections of values and practices within and across cultures and identities that he might call on, too. These intersections are neither essentialist nor all-encompassing nor universal; rather, they are produced and constrained differently in different contexts. The endless ways in which these intersectional identities and cultures might be in dialogue with one another create an infinite array of strategic intersectionalities that a self-in-dialogue might call on. For instance, this young man might evoke his cultural identity as a classical music lover and an army brat in one moment and that of an all-star baseball pitcher and a small town resident in another. Or his interest in digital photography and prolific Twitter use might lead him to consider images he would want to shoot to illustrate his burgeoning understandings of the text as it relates to his life.

Just as this young man may call on different intersectional identities to make sense of his life and the world around him, so too is he likely to experience multiple systems interrelating and bearing down on him in particular ways that make some intersectional identities more salient in a given moment than others. Oppression occurs when one group systematically and over a long period of time treats another group in unjust ways, often predictably, to deny another group access to societal resources like education, employment opportunities, social capital, economic stability, intellectual respect, criminal justice, and so on (Collins, 2000).

However, these "patterned treatments" (Leonardo, 2005) do not often bear down on a singular identity in isolation. For example, consider US wage gaps reported in 2014. Overall, women earned less than men across all races and ethnicities. But then take a look at intersectional identities: the median earnings per week for Asian women was $841; for White women, $703; for Black women $611; and for Latinas $548 (Bureau of Labor Statistics, 2014). The disparities widen within some groups if nationality or age or sexuality or marital status are taken into account. This is to say that systems—educational systems, employment systems, health systems, and the like—will often catch someone with an intersectional identity of a Latina single mother from Mexico differently than someone with a different intersectional identity. Further, the multiple systems a person navigates interconnect and weave together knotty systems of oppression that make some intersectional identities more salient for a person and differently subjugated than other intersectional identities that person may perform.

If we think back to the young Black man living in a small town, we might consider, for example, how local police might view this young man walking home in the evening. In that instance, the intersectional identity of his race and sex (male/female)—being a young Black man—is likely to be more salient to the officer and to the young man than his other possible intersectional identities. In the school locker room, others might view his intersectional identity as a gay Black man to be most salient even as he primarily experiences himself intersectionally in the locker room as a baseball player and a man. The ways different systems might bear down on these intersectional identities differently, and the ways this young man might in one moment give primacy to one of these intersections of self and in another moment foreground another intersection suggests something of the value-laden dynamism of the self-in-dialogue, both internally and externally.

The particular dynamics of the locker room or the classroom on that given day will also shape his responses, as will each new context he moves through. As this young man goes from his English class to shop class to AP Calculus to theater to a pep rally to after-school music lessons to baseball practice, what cultures are elevated or prized or disregarded by self and others in a moment? And how might each context, rife with constraints and possibility, help shape which of his cultures, which of his discourses or "identity kits" (Gee, 1990), which of his selves to project and which to downplay or merge with other parts of himself? How might he sift through an ever-changing range of cultural stances to know which ones to move through, linger in, or reshape in relation to people he might love, fear, enjoy, and/or need—people who are also navigating their own webs of multiple cultures?

The Purpose of the Book

Noted educator Maxine Greene wrote about what she called *emergent culture*, asserting that teachers need "to enable the diverse young to join the continually emergent culture's ongoing conversation" (1995, p. 56). Perhaps the only thing we, the authors, would change about Greene's statement is to move the apostrophe after the "s," to see *culture* as plural. We ask you to entertain this idea: humans construct *cultures*—that is, simultaneously more than one—and those *cultures* in turn construct individuals' identities and responses within contexts that are ever in flux. We argue that although any of us as individuals may in any given context represent ourselves more fully through the influence of one set of cultural experiences or practices, a range of other cultural experiences and practices remain in dialogue with that context.

In this book, we unpack some of the complexity of culture and identity, what people do with culture and identity, and how people navigate multiple cultures and multiple I-positions (Hermans & Hermans-Konopka, 2010). In essence, we're taking up questions about what to do with qualities, values, and experiences that are shared and what to do with difference wherever that shows up—within one person or among many. As an insistent part of people's daily lives, dialogues across culture occur routinely, often without any of us taking note. One of our intentions is to call these daily cultural transactions to the surface, to hold them up to the light, and to more consciously consider with you what doing so means for learning.

Later in the book, we'll spend some time unpacking and discussing culture and *cultures*, but for now, consider one way of thinking about how cultures work. As people share lives, experiences, concerns, and resources with others near and distant, they are shaped by and, in turn, shape what they share—values, materials, ways of being, relationships, institutions, and practices—and the ways they share these things with others. What is shared and how it is shared with others are what give rise to cultures that people find themselves part of, sometimes by choice, sometimes of necessity, sometimes by a bit of both. This assertion also suggests that cultures are marked and divided in this way: by what is shared—or perceived to be shared—in what ways, and by whom. Those who don't share, or can't share, or aren't allowed to share at all, or aren't allowed to share any longer or in the same way are often positioned, or position themselves, outside a culture.

Of course, such an understanding of cultures presents a binary: you're either in or you're out; you are either with the group or not with the group—and possibly against the group. In this book, we'll consider ideas about spectrums and intersections of cultural stances, but for now it is important to note that this kind of binary thinking is problematic, not only, but significantly because it's often too simplistic a schematic to take in the complex realities of a multicultural and multicontextual life. For example, Pablo Escobar, mastermind behind the Columbian drug cartel, was most likely responsible for the deaths of over 1,000 people. Yet, he also built schools, started hospitals, and advocated for the poor and political reform. Was he a good person or a bad person?

Or another example: Barack Obama has instituted a flawed but necessary health care initiative, has overseen a slow, but gradual recovery from economic recession, was instrumental in developing a world plan for coping with climate change that might be too little too late, and is likely responsible for killing at least as many innocent people as Pablo Escobar. Is he a good president or a bad president? On rare occasions, binaries might be useful ways of looking at issues in the world, but we usually find them lacking. They are too frequently used to justify facile and simplistic "solutions" to contexts that are far too complex and nuanced for such superficiality.

Yet such binary categorizing, so prevalent in so much of American politics, is too often perpetuated in our literacy classrooms. One sees it in the ways educators teach argument writing, where either/or thinking is perhaps most visible. It shows up when students are taught to create an airtight argument that is impervious to the ideas of others; when debates are cast in simplified win–loss terms; when difference that is different enough to breed uncertainty or conflict is seen as a threat, as something to be quieted or avoided.

dialogical self
"self-in-dialogue"

Revisiting the young man we mentioned earlier, it seems clear that he is navigating quite a bit of difference, difference that likely creates some degree of uncertainty or conflict in himself and/or in others around him. He experiences Black culture as part of his self, but also gay youth culture, Black Baptist culture, the culture of classical musicians, the culture of World of Warcraft players, the culture of online remix artists, the culture of military family life, the culture of the small, predominantly White town where he lives. Some of these cultures dialogue more easily with each other; some of these cultures are uneasy or even at odds with each other in the same self, in the same body, and differently at ease and at odds in different contexts. This young man has a self-in-dialogue, a dialogical self (Hermans & Hermans-Konopka, 2010), something we'll explore more in the coming pages.

As multicultural beings engaging in multicultural contexts, we dialogue both externally *and internally* with and through a range of cultural stances. When we do, those stances struggle to retain their integrity even as they shift to accommodate new understandings. When the young man's self-in-dialogue meets a classmate's self-in-dialogue or a teacher's self-in-dialogue, a host of cultures meet, with some intersections in some contexts more likely to open up and others more likely to close down dialogue, or at least certain elements of such dialogue.

What, then, do we who engage across cultural boundaries—that is to say, all of us—do when certain contexts or cultural stances or cultural experiences or cultural histories shape our transactions in a particular way—sometimes in predictably scripted ways—and yet there is some exigency to try to reconfigure those stances and those transactions? What might it mean in these contexts to reconfigure our ways with words by seeing our selves and the selves of others as dialogical—as multiple, in flux, in dialogue, unfinished? What is the role of literacy learning here when we need ways of sustaining solidarity and values we've long shared with others, *and* we need ways of listening and learning and building solidarity in new contexts with those we might not otherwise listen to and learn from, with those who might not otherwise listen to and learn from us? In this tension between solidarity and difference, between unity and fluidity lies tantalizing possibility and discomforting uncertainty. Within the extremes of those same tensions lies the dialogue that is this book.

Creating a Context for Dialoguing about Cultures and Selves

In writing this book and thinking about cultures, learning, literacy, and dialogical selves, two different experiences sprang to mind: 1) those times when we feel ourselves divided and say things like "Part of me thinks X, but part of me thinks Y" or "I don't know; I feel torn" and 2) those times when we feel the need to dig in our heels and hold our ground. In the practical world of everyday lives, these inclinations often occur when people most need to take action to get something worthwhile done, often with others who don't quite see eye-to-eye. In those cases, people need real ways of dialoguing across difference with their selves and with others, and they need ways of navigating complexity, uncertainty, and conflict that are productive and gain direction. As individuals, they need ways of using words with others that are open to unity and yet do not shy away from fluidity, difference, and possibility. As people in dialogue with the world around them, they need ways of moving with and through possible cultural stances that sustain integrity, accommodate uncertainty that creates a sense of "wobble" (Fecho, 2011; Garcia & O'Donnell-Allen, 2015) in their worldviews, and generate new understandings, new ways of being, new options and outcomes, new ways forward.

In this book, we hope to both validate and question your current conceptions of culture. We want you to see cultures as having been with you all your lives, but we want you to see them with new eyes. We want you to understand how in the United States, historically, the prevailing narrative has most often positioned individuals and groups via cultural stances and markers of insiders and outsiders around identity politics—political beliefs and formations that aim to secure political freedom of particular marginalized social and cultural groups—especially with relation to race and ethnicity. Then we want you to step outside that construct.

To do so, we ask you to think more expansively about cultures and cultural intersections, to also include cultures of cyclists; of transgender youth; of Midwestern towns; of bi-national border regions; of remix artists; of Future Farmers of America; of gamers; of basketball teams; of anime fans; of ROTC; of Catholics; of graffiti artists; of corporations like Google, Apple, Chic-Fil-A, Disney; of hybrid and mestizo/a cultures, and so on—and a vast range of possible combinations sometimes at home, sometimes at war in the same body. Some of these cultures we are born into; some we later join; some we take on temporarily; and some we invent, co-construct, or reinvent.

To help all of us in these efforts, we have constructed this book as a dialogue of sorts. Although pieces of this dialogue happened within the frenetic, but sometimes creative atmosphere of professional conferences devoted to educational issues, the bulk of it occurred via electronic means. In fact, we first knew each other strictly through various digital platforms. As readers of this text, you are most likely only coming to know us via the words on this page, therefore we think some personal, temporal, and spatial context would be useful at this point.

Bob's Story

I have been engaged in literacy education more than 40 years, beginning that career in 1974 as a junior high teacher in North Philadelphia. I went on to teach high school in the African-American communities of that city until 1998, when I started researching and teaching in language and literacy education at the University of Georgia. Although viewed as different through a socially constructed lens of race, I felt I had much in common with the Black adolescents I taught because, like them, I was raised in a working-class city neighborhood and well understood how language and poor-to-adequate K-12 schooling had colluded to keep people like us in our place.

However, my working-class upbringing in the 1950s also immersed me from an early age in all the overt and covert prejudices of that time. One of my earliest memories is gathering in a circle with other kids from the block, each with one foot thrust forward, and the leader thumping toes in succession as the group chanted, "Eeny, meeny, miney, moe." Sadly, what got caught in the next line was not the tiger of the more innocent version of that rhyme, but a nigger, although I am fairly certain that I was chanting that slur long before I could attach any meaning to the word. It was, at least at first, as nonsensical as "eeny" or "meeny," as were other derogatory terms often heard in the neighborhood like *fag, dike, kike,* and *wop.* Only the angry tones of 5-year-olds imitating older siblings or parents communicated the volatility behind those words. Such is the insidiousness of a cultural group bent on exclusion and preserving the status quo. It dresses in innocence and the commonplace its most vile conceptions.

In some ways, due to being raised in cities in the northeast US and having learned to teach in the Black communities of Philadelphia, I found teaching primarily young southern women, many from the wealthy suburbs around Atlanta, more of a cultural shift than my high school teaching experience. I remember a moment near the end of a course early in my UGA career when I was engaging in a discussion designed to help my undergraduates reflect on their experiences in the class. One young woman raised her hand and said that several of them were upset when I had yelled at them. Somewhat stunned, I couldn't remember any moments when I had yelled at the students. When they offered further explanation, I smiled somewhat in awareness and somewhat in amusement. "Oh," I said, "I remember now. No, I wasn't yelling. I was just being emphatic. You don't really want to hear me yell."

Still, despite my working class, Eastern European heritage being markedly different from the affluent class, Western European legacy that dominates so much of US culture, I also realized my status as a White, heterosexual, college-educated male accorded me many perks and benefits of the doubt. I can and frequently do pass for the White males of privilege who still dominate leadership in education, politics, and commerce. That is until I am among those alpha males who have grown up in generations of privilege and I am unmasked as not really being one of them. Maybe it's my lack of grace when confronted with titular authority, my unwillingness to wear a suit and tie at official functions, or my overt willingness to call absurd policy into question that reveals my differences. Or perhaps it's just my own self-awareness that my background and the values I've come to apply are often different from males of the dominant class and ethnic culture.

To an extent, my entire life has been spent doing what I call *reading culture.* Never feeling like I quite fit in—the working class boy who spent as much time in the library as he spent on the playing fields; the child raised Catholic who could never see the sense of worship; the White teacher among Black adolescents, the child of factory laborers attending and teaching in universities with the children of professionals—I have learned to look closely at the ways the cultures I entered functioned. As a result, I became fascinated by the deep and varied engagement with culture that all people experience.

Such border crossings haven't always been smooth or seamless, but, happily for me, when crossing boundaries of race, sexuality, gender, and even religion, those who have come to know me often sensed my openness toward cultures I was less familiar with, that I sought to develop a wider, more diverse understanding of the world. They have responded with support. I have always considered myself fortunate that when I have misspoken or awkwardly crossed a cultural boundary—as we all have at points in our lives—someone from that culture has, rather than reading me the riot act, taken the time to help me unlearn the cultural myths of my youth.

When the dialogue with Jen kicked into high gear, I typically worked from my office on the second floor of my home in Athens, Georgia. It's comfy in an Ikea sort of way, and strewn with artifacts of my life. A guitar amp sits next to a milk crate of books of educational literature. Blown-up photos of my granddaughter flank an equally large picture of my grandfather when he was a young man. A roller coaster made from a K'nex building set partially blocks access to my bookshelves. A black cat named Dipi who brooks no ignoring of her presence, competed for attention with the words on the laptop screen, as I one-finger typed my way through this book.

Jen's Story

In the early years of Bob's career in Philadelphia, I was growing up in a working-class family in Savannah, Georgia, making periodic visits to see my father, a farmer in a poor rural area a couple of hours away. A volatile home life that most often crushed difference and alternative orientations—left-handedness, introversion, a progressive Christianity, queerness—set the stage for a career considering what we do with each other's differences. My fierce athleticism and agility so prized on the basketball court only invoked rage when that same dexterity spilled out in an edgy sense of humor or a too bold observation of things my family didn't want to talk about. A private school education funded by basketball scholarships helped me pass, occasionally, as middle class, but the ways I didn't or couldn't conform in my home, kept me always wary, even in my own insider cultures, sometimes especially there.

In many ways, I felt more at home with the working class youth I taught and coached decades later in north Georgia—African American, Latino/a, and White—so obviously and beautifully on the cusp of so many messy worlds—surprisingly adult one moment and surprisingly young the next and sometimes oddly and seamlessly both at the same time. Later, in Arizona and Missouri and Texas, the grit and struggle, the kinship and ceremony of the South Sudanese diasporic communities, indigenous nations, and LGBTQ youth I worked with often resonated more with me than the cultures of White, hetero-normative middle-class students and teachers I came to know. I grew to trust the reliability of difference, a recognizable outsider-ness and a sometimes explicitly negotiated insider-ness more than unspoken assumptions of commonality.

And yet, I realized that my Whiteness and the historical dominance of a pre-dominately White South and of White middle-class school systems had afforded me opportunities and status that worked, mostly, for my gain. I also realized that my ability to pass as mainstream—even among queer friends and colleagues—and to perform a particular version of gender typically coded as female bought me safety and the invisibility of the normal that hetero-normative friends, family, and colleagues didn't question.

When colleagues at the University of Missouri suggested that my scholarship seemed to resonate deeply with Bob's work, I sent Bob an email introducing myself. Both of us quickly recognized mutual interests in writing, dialogue, and dialogical pedagogy, social justice issues, and culture. Wanting space we both could access easily and use as a repository for our dialogue, we opened a blog site and began to exchange ideas.

In conversation with Bob, I often worked from my home office, situated in El Paso, Texas, on a slope at the foot of the Rockies overlooking the Chihuahuan Desert. Jasper, a lovely nutjob of a rescue dog, alternately sleeps, whines, looks out the windows, and begs me to play ball. A train whistle sounds, cueing the neighborhood dogs to bark and howl in chorus. I do a kind of strategic multitasking: responding to a blog, pulling up references and sites that come to mind, and occasionally responding to an i-message from friends across the country.

Of course, what it means for me to be queer, Christian, and White here in El Paso, where I am a minority in a Latino/a, borderland, primarily conservative Catholic environment, is quite different than what it meant earlier in my life and in different settings. Even in Georgia, what it meant for me to be queer in north Georgia, away from my family, was quite different than what it meant in Savannah with my family, where they do not know that I am queer or have a partner—a decision I experience as a painfully complicated form of love and wisdom and protection and one I'm sure some of my family would experience as layered betrayal. Missouri was the first time that I was part of a church where I felt it was safe to be openly queer among strangers and where others didn't think being queer somehow cut me off from being Christian. In that church, I could explore and perform a dialogue between being Christian and being queer differently than I ever had before. Prior to that, I experienced deep acts of violence by some of my closest friends and by institutions where I hoped to feel safe.

Dialoguing Together

Writing together now, we have found the back and forth, the unexpected departures, the push-back, the solidarity, the wobble, the questions and reinventions of our dialogue to be productive for wrestling with ideas of cultures, dialogues, literacy, learning, agency, and dialogical selves and especially for thinking about what these ideas mean for teachers and for youth. In a book about cultures in dialogue, we've tried to stay as true to the nature of dialogue—at least the nature of our dialogue—as possible. Our initial emails and blogs have evolved into this text, one that was written in a give-and-take process between the two of us, with hopeful starts and incomplete drafts commuting the electronic distance between our laptops. It is through these processes that this book was generated. Sometimes one of us would write and the other would respond the next day. At other times, weeks would pass before our busy academic lives allowed us time for the next response. But slowly, if not steadily, a rich dialogue about culture, learning, and the dialogical self began to form between us.

Of course, the settings in which we write sound a bit more serene than the ways we actually experience the internal and external borderlands we find ourselves navigating as we make our way in the dialogue that is this book. It is no coincidence that these paragraphs about our own cultures and selves-in-dialogue were the last paragraphs we inserted into this introduction, despite the paragraphs seemingly yet to come. We knew we would need to include our own dialogues and dissonance as part of our social contract with you as readers, and we knew that our dialogue with you would be richer for it. Even so, we were happy to put off the wobbling that might be caused by the writing of these paragraphs as long as we could. Wobble is, after all, a very personal thing.

As we began writing together, we experienced our multiple cultures in dialogue with each other, with our past selves, with our present selves, with the future selves we're constructing. Sometimes we felt an easy fit, for example, with our working-class values. Sometimes we experienced a taut line like those first moments of tug-of-war when pulling in different directions keeps people on their feet and the rope steady. Of course, we aren't in any way at war, but the tension of our dialogues has been at times both valuable and real. Sometimes we find ourselves surprised and full of wonder and in a state of not knowing, a state of shared listening, as I (Jen) learn of Bob's Eastern European or northeastern US or musical cultures or as I (Bob) learn of Jen's experiences with basketball or Navy cultures.

Sometimes we also find ourselves wondering about and anticipating your cultural responses, and we try to account for our Whiteness as a social construct tied to material benefits even as we try to expand our and your understandings of cultures as something beyond ethnicity and nationality. Our dialogue was—still is—both invigorating in its shared stances, yet creatively unsettling in its differences. It is into this dialogue that we invite you, in hopes that together we might build and refine our theories about how cultures, literacies, and selves *actually* dialogue and how they *could* dialogue with each other in our lives and in our classrooms.

Of course, our theories—those of all who try to make meaning—need to *work* (Clifton, 2013). If they matter at all, our working theories matter because they are born in a space of felt difficulty, because of "some real-world need, some palpable contradiction" (Spellmeyer, 1993, p. 185) that makes our questions meaningful and worthwhile in the first place. In asking those questions, in responding to the many ways others respond to us, we engage both in a process of building and working out our theories *and* in a process of putting them to use and testing them to see if and how they work, if they hold. In this way, all of our theories are, to a greater or lesser extent, in the process of being worked out.

At its best, our theory building in the face of what doesn't (yet) make sense or what doesn't (yet) work opens up possibility and leads to framing and reframing action. This kind of grounded theory building calls on us to do something, to run our theory through someone else's gauntlet and see if and how it shapes up on the other side. That is, the real test of a working theory is, well, that it *works*: that "it is operational (a tool kit of conditions and strategies); it is situated (adapted to its particular time, place, and people); and it is always under revision (responding to the test of outcomes)" (Flower, 2008, p. 90). It is this work that we most hope you will take up with us in this book.

WORKING THEORIES: DIALOGUE AND PRAGMATISM

In the interest of dialogue, we've included a number of sidebar conversations throughout the book, wherever they might feel apt. These conversations either occurred in the margins of drafts or in separate emails. Whatever topic they take up, these sidebars bear witness to the ongoing dialogue that allowed this text to be written, a dialogue that sometimes had us taking different stances or holding diverse understandings on key terms or beliefs. In this sidebar, we take up our different thoughts related to the notion of a *working theory*. We raise this exchange here because even in seemingly small exchanges over wording, our dialogical selves were at work making sense of the text at hand and of the ways we negotiate our individual and shared commitments.

Framing the Dialogue (Bob)

As I was reading what was then the most recent draft sent to me by Jen, I came across her insertion about working theory. Assuming we had a common understanding of the term, I added a sentence that suggested that *working theory* was redundant, in that, for me, all theories undergo constant reshaping as new contexts are encountered. Below is our margin dialogue that followed.

Jen: I hear what you're saying here, but this is a place where we differ, I think. I'm using working theory here in a way that indicates our theorizing informs our actions in a constrained world. The comment about working and theory being redundant seems dismissive – even though I don't necessarily think that's what you intend – and undercuts a body of knowledge in rhetoric about theory building and pragmatism...

Bob: Regarding working theory, my understanding of the general use of the term is that it's a theory in process, that it could be substantially changed or replaced. Googling the term, it seems to be the most common use. When I read what you wrote, I wasn't sure if you were playing with words or if you really wanted it to be a theory that is, in fact, working, doing what it purports to do. Or, as your comment indicates, you might be using the term based upon theoretical lit that I'm not familiar with. Regardless, just toss what I wrote, although I do think you need to be more explicit that you're using the term in a way that's different from the more common use of that expression.

Jen's Take

Initially, Bob's changes sought to *clarify* a shared meaning of *working theory*. Those clarifications revealed, to me at least, that we did not necessarily have a shared understanding; we would need to construct one. To build something, to some degree, shared, we would need to articulate our differences. Bob's changes seemed to me like an undoing of the rough ground of theory-building and of the precise rhetorical work and hopeful pragmatism I had in mind—the very things I think matter most in our theory building. We act on our theories. And yet, when we are theorizing how our world in flux works, what our place is in a changing world, what is most needed, what we might do ... there is a lot we cannot be sure of, a lot we cannot reliably achieve no matter how precise we are in representing a complex situation to ourselves and in constructing wise action with others. It's precisely when our lives are most uncertain, most constrained that we most urgently need our theories, always tentative, in progress, and perspectival, to *work*—to actually produce the version of health we had in mind and hoped for. A grounded urgency demands our best actionable knowledge.

What Bob couldn't have known at the time—or indeed until the writing of this sidebar after we completed the full text of the book—is that the fierceness and commitment I have to a prophetic pragmatism (Flower, 1994, 2002, 2008; Gilyard, 2008, 2011; Flower, Long, & Higgins, 2000; Peck, Flower, & Higgins, 1995; West, 2005) informing *working theories* (Flower, 2008) stems from lived experiences in which I and others I care about deeply have needed our risky theories to hold and come through for us and for others. It stems equally from deep solidarity with disciplinary colleagues up to the gritty and contested work of building a deep democracy (Gilyard, 2008, 2011; West, 2005) that values differences of all kinds, prizes individuality, and fosters wise action as well as systematic interrogation of shared values, common practices, and unevenly distributed power—especially when we are most constrained and most uncertain. That is, these intellectual commitments are also deeply personal, relational, and historical—informing, issuing from, and constructing anew many of my own ongoing dialogues.

Bob's Take

And I come not from that world. My grasp of the term *working theory* was constructed completely from a nonacademic stance. Unlike the term *transaction*, which we discuss in the next chapter's sidebar, I was not deeply invested in the concept of working theory. In fact, the reason I web searched the term is because I really wasn't completely sure what was generally meant by it, and was seeking confirmation from a range of sources. My statement regarding the idea that using *working* to modify *theory* seemed redundant was not meant to be dismissive, but more an attempt to align the concept with my stance that context is a change agent, that what appears one way in one context often appears differently in others.

What I hope is a takeaway here is that even among people with whom you share a close working and theoretical relationship, you can't assume that your base understandings of terms are always in agreement. Instead, shades, gaps, or even chasms of meaning difference might exist. Unless such differences are brought to the surface, you will stumble on with the mistaken notion that what you consider something to mean and what experiences you have brought to bear on that meaning are shared. I think the text reveals that, through our unpacking of *working theory*, we were able to construct a discussion that worked for both of us.

As you read about our cultures and identities, your own stories likely come to mind. We invite you to take some time to think about the cultures that shaped your early understandings of yourself and of others. What form did that take? Was it through particular words, through images, through stories or films? You might also consider when you might have felt uneasy with those formative cultures. When did you experience some rub or tension between cultures you found yourself part of, or wanting to be part of? Can you remember a time when those tensions were especially salient? Was your dialogue with these cultures primarily internal or external or some combination? Where did you find yourself being more open to these dialogues? Where did you find yourself more closed? And what did you do when you experienced a dialogue as more open or more closed? Odds are, if your experience is anything like ours, some of the experiences that come to mind bring a bit of liveliness or reassurance and others quite a bit of vulnerability or wobble. We know that these experiences and ongoing dialogues are seldom tidy, but we hope that you will come to rest assured that they can be quite productive.

Sketching the Landscape of the Book

As we think should happen in any good dialogue—where dialogue is about knowing, not knowing, and coming to know newly—this book emerged from our questions. In response to our years of attempting to navigate and weave together the complexities, the uncertainties, and the values of dialogical teaching, we began to construct a list of framing questions that we hoped might, at first, focus our dialogue and, ultimately, focus this book.

The obvious question—what is culture, or what do we mean by the term culture—jumped up first and large, perhaps too large. We found the question really too big for our purposes. As I (Jen) noted on our blog:

> Admittedly, [defining culture] at first feels like I've bitten off more than I can chew, I suppose, because [capital] C-culture is such a nebulous, elusive idea. I best know the cultures I'm part of in the doing, in the being, and at the outer edges where I might share or borrow a friend's cultural ways of being or where I might experience tension and ill-ease when one set of cultural values and practices doesn't easily mesh with another set.

Trying to comprehensively define capital C Culture would take us down a rabbit hole and tunnel us into areas that, although not uninteresting and significant, would distract us from our main purpose of contemplating the ways cultures shape our educational lives and how those educational lives, in turn, shape cultures. Furthermore, by providing too incisive a discussion about culture, we run the risk of stabilizing too much something that is always in flux and of predetermining your interpretations of what our mutual dialogue with you might yield.

Those reluctances noted, some general framework regarding how we will be using the concept of *culture* in our work serves to create, at the least, a starting point for our continued refining of our understandings. To this end, we juxtapose two descriptions of culture—one by noted multicultural educator Sonia Nieto and the second by the literature scholar Edward Said. Both are broad enough yet precise enough to guide our thinking about what we mean when we write of *culture*. And both descriptions implicate the complex ways cultures weave within our lives.

In 1992, Nieto explained that culture was "the ever-changing values, traditions, social and political relationships, and worldview created, shared, and transformed by a group of people bound together by a combination of factors that can include

culture

Nieto ∆ *Said*

Culture – dynamic

a common history, geographic location, language, social class, and religion" (as cited in Nieto, 2010, p. 136). What particularly stands out to us in this description of culture is how, as quickly as the second word, Nieto stated that culture is in no way static. Furthermore, she was careful to qualify what construes culture, noting what *can* be included as opposed to what is. In what we interpret as purposeful ambiguity, Nieto has outlined a construction of culture that can be read as an all-encompassing capital C Culture or, more in line with our stances, a rich web of constantly intersecting cultures. To that latter end, Nieto (2010) enhanced this discussion by asserting that culture is dynamic, multifaceted, contextual, sociocul-turally influenced and constructed, learned, and tension filled. Although we would add that culture is frequently acquired, or learned in ways that aren't always obvi-ous and overt (Gee, 2012), we feel this definition makes explicit the dynamics and complexity inherent in the construction of culture.

For his purposes, Edward Said is perhaps best known for his work interrogat-ing how power is perpetuated through culture. Said, a Palestinian American cul-tural critic, who grew up in a family of Palestinian Christians in the Middle East, analyzed how people of the Western world perceive and represent people and things of a different culture. In particular, he wrote that these representations are related to power dynamics, to the ways one culture positions itself in relation to another culture, and to implicit justifications for ongoing colonial and imperial actions. In writing about culture and imperialism, Said connected culture to aes-thetic forms like literature, songs, paintings, dance, clothing, sculptures, cartoons, newspapers, and jokes. Said (1994) explained that these forms can reveal a lot about the stories that we come to believe about ourselves and about others, about how we come to believe those narratives, and how we come to reproduce and live out those narratives.

Said also noted that "almost imperceptibly, culture is a concept that includes a refining and elevating element, each society's reservoir of the best that has been known and thought"(1994, p. xii). Importantly, Said discussed the ways this "ele-vating element" is both valuable and dangerous: valuable in the ways we come to learn from the best of our cultures—from Dante and Shakespeare, as he noted for example; dangerous in that the "best" cultural artifacts are often seen as separate from the cultural politics of our everyday lives and in that we can sometimes insist on a "best" that denigrates or doesn't agree with or doesn't allow the "best" of other cultures.

As Nigerian author Chimamanda Adichie (2009) warned, there is danger in a single story. When those with the power to do so canonize a book or any work of art, they act at the exclusion of other works and thus obscure, obfuscate, or even obliterate other stories, perspectives, and worldviews. For example, as classroom teachers we might include Anglo-American or British classics in literature classes, but, as was legislated in Arizona's SB1070 ban of ethnic studies, we might not include classics of indigenous American, African-American, or Luso-American literature. And we might not associate prizing our Anglo literary canon in classrooms as at all informing or connected to whom we prize in and beyond our classrooms. Or we might discuss narratives of classics from a range of cultural traditions but not engage dialogue about relevant contemporary narratives as they are bearing out in people's day-to-day lives.

Consider these instances. In the fall of 2014, when the racial protests in Missouri—the home of Mark Twain—were at their height and all over the national news, the National Council of Teachers of English, concerned that policymakers might be stifling dialogue, asked teachers if they were allowed to talk in their classrooms about the protests. In another ongoing struggle, teachers in school districts across the country navigate unspoken policies to sidestep anything related to homosexuality—in health classes, in English classes, in history classes, in the hallways, and in the cafeterias. In these cases, the narratives and cultural artifacts explored in classrooms that could provide a provocative basis for dialogue across cultures—say race relations in *Huck Finn* or romantic relationships and gender roles in *Taming of the Shrew*—are too frequently elevated above the fray of our everyday lives.

Although such works can and, we think, should be taught in ways that encourage young readers to engage the texts' connections and disconnections with their lives, our experience indicates they are too often taught as if they existed in worlds unto themselves—worlds not only far removed but also largely inconsequential to youth, or at least inconsequential to particular youth. Curiously, their being taught in seeming vacuums does little to lessen their impact on learners. The sheer weight of all that White, male, heterosexual, and elite class literature is deeply and insidiously powerful, whether or not readers see the characters and contexts and plot lines of those works directly connected to the lives they lead and the cultures they construct. After all, we who teach and youth, like the young man we mentioned earlier, are still navigating the cultures of our classrooms *and* the many cultures we transact with beyond the classroom. Our selves-in-dialogue keep dialoguing internally and externally, whether we make these dialogues the subject of education or not.

Given the framework of these definitions, given what they entail and with what consequence, what, we wondered, happens to us daily as we transact with and within a range of cultures? We were particularly interested in knowing what happens when I-positions—what psychologists Hubert Hermans and Angieszka Hermans-Konopka (2010) describe as those many manifestations of culture that populate the more or less cohesive identity we present to the world—dialogue across each other and with the many cultural contexts we encounter daily. If cultural transactions are omnipresent, what happens during our day-to-day negotiations across cultural boundaries, particularly within educational settings? How are we as individuals shaping and being shaped by these ongoing transactions?

These questions brought us to what we see as the multicultural self—a self shaped by multiple cultures, a self-in-dialogue with multiple cultures, a self enacting

[handwritten margin note: Subcultures – what happens to them w/ many cultural encounters within the classroom?]

a "multicultural self"

multiple cultures, a self shaping multiple cultures. A person's cultural transactions—
simultaneous, complex, ongoing, and fluid—reveal a self-in-dialogue. But how
do these dialogues occur? Not always in back-and-forth conversations; in fact,
there are jokes about talking to yourself: it's okay as long as you don't answer
back, the punch line goes.

How do dialogues/convos work?
DST
dialogical self theory

How does it work, then? How have these dialogical selves been theorized?
One prominent theory that we will explore more in this book is Hermans and
Hermans-Konopka's (2010) dialogical self theory (DST). We'll unpack this theory
as it relates to culture, learning, identity, and dialogue throughout the book, but
for now a brief explanation will be helpful. Dialogical self theory brings the concepts of "self" and "dialogue" together in profound ways. In psychology, the self
has often been considered primarily internal and singular, housed in the mind of
an individual person. Dialogue, on the other hand, has primarily been considered
an external process of communication among more than one individual. The
DST veers away from a self–other dichotomy and instead considers the "dialogical
self," which engages in both internal and external dialogue. In DST, the self is
extended not just into the world, but *dialogically* into the world just as the world
is extended *dialogically* into the self.

Further, the dialogical self is composed of multiple I-positions within a single
self. These I-positions are both internal (I as an athlete, I as a homebrew maker,
I as my mom's daughter) and external (fellow cyclist, fellow teacher, part of the
classes I teach, family member, group member). There is, then, no sharp divide
between internal and external selves or internal and external dialogues. There is,
rather, a gradual and perhaps hazy transition as our internal and external worlds
intersect and transact in ways so that the other is seen as a constituent part of the
self.

As educators, we wonder what dialogical self theory has to say about ways
these dialogues might be productive, internally and externally? How might DST
help teachers and youth imagine ways to respond to the complexities of the
technology-driven and globalized world we live in, where cultural transactions are
linked and quickened in ways that weren't possible just a few decades, even a few
years ago? What access and agency does DST provide for coping with tensions
and uncertainties caused in the contact zones (Pratt, 1991) of multiple cultural
transactions? Finally, what does all this dialogue about culture mean for teachers
and students, and for the classrooms they mutually construct and inhabit? How
can we as educators construct dialogical stances not only in our classrooms but
also with colleagues, parents, administrators, and others who hold a stake in the
support and enhancement of public schools?

contact zones

What to Expect from This Book

In the five chapters that follow this introduction, we urge you to dialogue with us
about cultures (Chapter 1), learning (Chapter 2), literacy (Chapter 3), identity

(Chapter 4), and agency (Chapter 5). Neither of us can imagine a functioning classroom that respects the learning process that does not address the complex ways these five factors touch, mesh, clash, confront, engage, obstruct, and involve one another in the substantive construction of meaning. Within the complexity of literacy classrooms, teachers and youth engage in multiple dialogical transactions that continue to shape who they are becoming and how they will construct themselves within as well as how they will construct the cultures we encounter daily.

In our lives and in our classrooms, these five factors are difficult, if not impossible, to tease apart from one another in the moment. That point noted, throughout the rest of the book, we rely on writing as a way to stabilize and isolate—just momentarily—particular factors to explore and reflect on the ways they work together and on the ways we transact with them. In order to do this, we borrow an organizational concept from the creators of *The Wire,* the HBO drama about the complex ways race, class, and social institutions clash in urban America. The first season of that series was focused on law enforcement and drug trafficking in Baltimore's most depressed neighborhoods. The second season kept its focus on drug dealing and policing, but brought in the complexity of the effect of dying industries on unions. Organized labor, police, and drug dealers figured into season three with the added layer of local politics. Season four retained all of the above, but highlighted education and season five rounded out the series with the spotlight on media.

In a similar fashion, we start the book with a discussion of cultures and the dialogical self. Over the course of the book we gradually build to consider learning, literacy, identity, and agency. Throughout, we contemplate what it means to have selves in dialogue and what it might mean to support the dialogical selves of the young people we care so much about, and to do it in ways that do justice to the complexity, uncertainty, and meaning making of our everyday lives.

In Chapter 1, we deepen the discussion of cultures and the dialogical self that we've started in this introduction. In addition to firming up our argument for our conception of cultures plural rather than culture singular, we also seek to blur the hard line between internal and external cultures. In doing so, we unpack the idea of a multivoiced, dialogical self and consider the multiple ways we dialogue with cultures—from the immediately palpable to the ambient—internally and externally. By considering dialogue from a range of perspectives, our intent is to create some interesting places to name and think about what we do with uncertainty and difference and how we gain direction in an increasingly pluralistic and connected, but complex world.

Chapter 2 considers the implications of all we've discussed to this point for education writ large. We are especially interested in the differences between being educated and being schooled, and how some of us embrace education and learning, but do not necessarily embrace school. Or how the cultures of schools often act as winnowing devices that sift adolescents into slots not necessarily of their choosing and from which they rarely find escape. Additionally, we draw on cognitive dissonance and suggest that dialogue in such instances is a starting point for substantive learning. It is in such moments of wobble, when the disequilibrium seems greatest, that immersing in dialogue and inquiry become ways for navigating through the uncertainty toward newly constructed understandings that offer at least a momentary sense of stability.

We add literacy into the mix in Chapter 3. In doing so, we bring meaning making—textual, visual, material, mediated, performative, and so on—to the forefront. We are particularly concerned with the way literacies transact with cultures in and out of school, and in and among our multicultural dialogical selves. What is the role of literacy within educational contact zones for reproducing and reconstructing cultures, for participating in and engaging with cultures, for reshaping and revaluing cultures and selves in dialogue? How can learners take what literacy affords in terms of raising and posing questions, in terms of making sense of competing ideas or selves or values, and in terms of generating new knowledge that somehow takes competing ideas seriously? Importantly, we discuss the tensions, uncertainty, and power issues that undoubtedly occur in classrooms where cultures, literacies, and the dialogical selves are transacting.

All of the dialogical transactions we've discussed in the previous chapters have been in service of Chapter 4's focus—identity creation. When we think about identity in relation to these other ideas, how do we think about becoming—about what it might mean to see ourselves and others in various states of becoming? Literacy theorist Paulo Freire (1970) has suggested that humans exist in a perpetual state of incompleteness while Bakhtin (1984) has written about how language gains us a place at the table in a "feast of becoming" (p. 10). In the eyes of both theorists, we are always constructing self in relation to other. In doing so, we are refining, generating, limiting, embracing, troubling, and engaging the many I-positions within us. During this lifelong process, we present identities to ourselves and others that are simultaneously fully formed and under construction, cohesive and fractured, predicated on the past and predicated on the future, and somehow responsive to the unfolding present.

Finally, in Chapter 5, we more intently consider the agency of teachers, students, and teacher educators as we return to questions of power: so what *do* we *do* in these dialogical transactions? What are the ways we're already being shaped and what does it mean to shape our selves, our literacies, our education, our cultures? What does it mean for teachers to dialogue with colleagues, with parents, with administrations, with the public, and with policymakers? In particular, we suggest that the issues that affect classrooms and schools are extremely complex and, in being so, are less given to solutions and more responsive to directions to be explored, followed, and then reflected upon. In this concluding chapter, we provide possible ways for contending with the wobble and uncertainty that our contending with diversity brings, knowing full well that such sharing of ideas is only provocation for more and hopefully better dialogues to come.

References

Adichie, C. (2009, July). "Chimamanda Ngozi Adichie: The danger of a single story." [Video file]. Retrieved from https://www.ted.com/talks/chimamanda_adichie_the_danger_of_a_single_story?language=en

Bakhtin, M. (1984). *Rabelais and his world.* Helene Iswolsky, Trans. Bloomington, IN: U of Indiana Press. (Original work published 1965.)

Bureau of Labor Statistics. (2014). Highlights of women's earnings in 2014. [Data file.] Retrieved from http://www.bls.gov/opub/reports/cps/highlights-of-womens-earnings-in-2014.pdf

Clifton, J. (2013). Mastery, failure, and community outreach as a stochastic art: Lessons learned with the Sudanese diaspora in Phoenix. In J. Restaino and L. J. Cella (Eds.) *Unsustainable: Re-imagining community literacy, public writing, service learning, and the university* (pp. 227–52). New York: Lexington Books.

Collins, P. H. (2000). *Black feminist thought: Knowledge, consciousness, and the politics of empowerment.* Florence, KY: Psychology Press.

Fecho, B. (2011). *Teaching for the students: Habits of heart, mind, and practice in the engaged classroom.* New York: Teachers College Press.

Flower, L. (1994). *The construction of negotiated meaning: A social cognitive theory of writing.* Carbondale: Southern Illinois Press.

Flower, L. (2002). Intercultural knowledge building: The literate action of a community think tank. In C. Bazerman and D. Russell (Eds.) *Writing selves/Writing societies: Research from activity perspectives.* Fort Collins, CO: The WAC Clearinghouse. Retrieved from: http://wac.colostate.edu/books/selves_societies/

Flower, L. (2008). *Community literacy and the rhetoric of public engagement.* Carbondale, IL: Southern Illinois University Press.

Flower, L., Long, E., and Higgins, L. (2000). *Learning to rival: A literate practice for intercultural inquiry.* New York: Routledge.

Freire, P. (1970). *Pedagogy of the oppressed.* Myra Bergman Ramos, Trans. New York: Continuum Publishing Company.

Garcia, A., and O'Donnell-Allen, C. (2015). *Pose, wobble, flow: A culturally proactive approach to literacy instruction.* New York: Teachers College Press.

Gee, J. (1990). *Social linguistics and literacies: Ideology in discourses.* New York: Routledge.

Gee, J. P. (2012). *Social linguistics and literacies: Ideology in discourses* (4th edition). New York: Routledge.

Gilyard, K. (2008). *Composition and Cornel West: Notes toward a deep democracy.* Carbondale: Southern Illinois Press.

Gilyard, K. (2011). *True to the language game: African American discourse, cultural politics.* New York: Routledge.

Greene, M. (1995). *Releasing the imagination: Essays on education, the arts, and social change.* San Francisco: Jossey-Bass.

Hermans, H., and Hermans-Konopka, A. (2010). *Dialogical self theory: Positioning and counter-positioning in a globalizing society.* Cambridge: Cambridge UP.

Leonardo, Z. (2005). The color of supremacy: Beyond the discourse of "white privilege." In Z. Leonardo (Ed.) *Critical pedagogy and race* (pp. 37–52). Malden, MA: Blackwell Publishing.

Nieto, S. (2010). *Language, culture, and teaching: Critical perspectives.* New York: Routledge.

Pascoe, C. J. (2007). *Dude, you're a fag.* Berkeley, CA: UC Press.

Peck, W. C., Flower, L., and Higgins, L. (1995). Community literacy. *College Composition and Communication*. National Council of Teachers of English. 46(2), 199–222.

Pratt, M. L. (1991). Arts of the contact zone. *Profession*, 91, 33–40.

Said, E. (1994). *Culture and imperialism*. New York: Vintage Books.

Spellmeyer, K. (1993). *Common ground: Dialogue, understanding and the teaching of composition*. Englewood Cliffs: Prentice-Hall.

West, C. (2005). *Democracy matters: Winning the fight against imperialism*. New York: Penguin.

1

CULTURES AND THE DIALOGICAL SELF

"Well, it's all a bit complicated."

Bob was sitting in a coffee shop with a colleague—we'll call her Connie—trying to convince her to co-facilitate a summer writing institute with him. Connie continued, "I really want to do the institute—I mean, it's a great opportunity—but we're a one-car family and I live on the eastside. If I drive to the institute, I basically confine my husband and son to the house all day, or I'll have to get them up way early and make them drive me and pick me up later, which doesn't seem fair."

Connie took a breath, "Plus I'm working on a book project with this great co-author I met online—we finish each other's sentences—and I need to carve out time to work on that." She paused and stared out the window, as if imagining other possibilities. "But it's been so long since I wrote poetry and the institute would let me feed that side of myself."

In looking back at this conversation, we believe Connie's situation is a vivid illustration of how the various I-positions that contribute to our ongoing identity construction engage in dialogue that is simultaneously internal and external. We have been tossing this term *I-positions* around but want to begin unpacking our orientation to its meaning here, an orientation we will continue to deepen and nuance throughout the book.

According to Hermans and Hermans-Konopka (2010), "collective voices speak through the mouth of the individual person" (p. 6). In a given moment, individuals echo, construct, and transform the many cultures they carry with them in that interaction, speaking with one voice and yet shaping and being shaped by many. In this way, all of us on this planet participate in and come in contact with a range of cultures throughout our daily experience. The various positions we construct in relation to those cultures reside and continue to fluctuate within each of us.

As multicultural beings living in multicultural contexts, our cultural dialogues are not just external or just internal and external, but internally external and externally internal. Put another and less paradoxical way, as cultures outside you engage in dialogue and cultures within you engage in dialogue, those cultures within us and outside us engage in dialogue in a blurred space, sometimes more external and other times more internal. As Hermans and Hermans-Konopka (2010) phrase it, "the other is not outside the self, but rather an intrinsic part of it" (p. 7).

Returning to Connie, one stance she takes is that of a literacy educator who would enjoy working with teachers in an intensive 18-day summer institute devoted to writing and writing instruction. Then there's Connie the mother and Connie the wife, neither of whom wants to put husband and son to too much inconvenience. Her husband and son are not only outside her self and part of her external life but also deeply internalized within Connie's imagination as part of who she is. Another I-position—Connie as co-author—feels responsible to honor a commitment to collaborate on a project with someone whose work and ways of working resonate with hers. Yet that more academic voice is tempered by Connie the poet who would enjoy having the broad expanse of the summer institute to indulge herself in the insightful verse she writes so well.

There are less obvious, but equally compelling dialogues occurring here concurrently. How Connie views herself as an independent woman who is self-employed and primary income producer for her family teeters against patriarchal vestiges of what constitutes good mothering and female spousal support. Perhaps beliefs about productivity—the 60-hour work ethic so prominent in the US—voice concerns about her wanting to indulge in an art form. She considers herself someone who is a good collaborator and sensitive to the needs of others—husband, son, co-author—but also wants to, perhaps even needs to develop an emotional, aesthetic facet in her life. And these are only the dialogues that became most evident in the short discussion about the teaching gig. Who knows what other I-positions may have entered the internal discussion, but never made it to the external dialogue.

hidden I-positions

Sketching the Dialogue of Cultures

"dialogue of cultures"

We can say that people live in a clash of cultures. Or we could say people live in a mesh of cultures. Others might call it a hybridity of cultures. Still others, a dovetailing of cultures, or a crush of cultures, or a diversity of cultures. In this book, we suggest that all of us exist and constantly transact in a dialogue of cultures.

To start, what do we mean when we type the word *dialogue*? Although both of us have read extensively in and believe passionately about the liberatory literacy work of Brazilian educator Paulo Freire (1970), we are not referencing his vision of dialogue, at least not as key and center to our discussions in this text. Freirean dialogue occurs only under certain conditions and at the volition of those involved in the dialogical situation. Conditions must be met, among them being that those who oppress and those who are oppressed need to help each other create new ways of transacting, to not merely trade places.

Instead, much of our conception of dialogue springs from the work of Russian literary theorist Mikhail Bakhtin. To embrace Bakhtinian (1981, 1986) dialogical theory is to embrace the inevitability of tension being present in our lives. He argued that language is continuously beset by centripetal tensions—unifying, but eventually reifying—and centrifugal tensions—individualizing, but eventually disuniting. As the prior sentence implies, we need language to be both unified and individual. It's not a question of one force or the other; rather, the tensions should create a humming, mutually energizing buzz that is only possible where more than one force is present and in productive, dynamic resistance with the others.

Being too skewed toward either uniformity or individualism is problematic; Instead, relatively equal forces pushing and tugging at each other can give direction, and redirection, to shared meanings needed to create a healthy language, society, or personality. In the rough ground and the taut pull of dynamic tensions, we seek—at least to an extent and perhaps temporarily—common agreement, or equilibrium, in our shared meanings so that communication can be facilitated. Yet we simultaneously imbue words with our own meanings—ones both nuanced and widely variant—pushing and pulling even upon those shared meanings as they, too, shift in response to the context in which meaning is being made.

As Bakhtin (1981) noted, language is something that is given to us—it comes with the touch of others—but, in our giving it back, we color it, shade it, shape it, spin it in ways that leave our fingerprints on it. Take a simple and common word like *pitch* and run it through its range of meanings: a tar-like substance, a thrown ball, a cricket field, a slope, a proposal, a measure of tone, a degree of alignment, a level of intensity. As a verb, we pitch a tent, a fit, a baseball, an idea, or an attack. As any word—in this case, *pitch*—undergoes centripetal and centrifugal tensions, its uses and meanings shift, with new meanings coming to play and other meanings losing sway, but not completely disappearing.

Furthermore, all these meanings are subject to context. We only understand *pitch* as a thrown ball if the context—perhaps a major league baseball game—suggests that meaning. The combination of the word and the context tug those in conversation toward a unified meaning. However, if one of those in conversation at the ballpark is an Australian and referred to the playing area as a pitch, much as he would a cricket field, his American baseball buddies might, at least at first, be confused. The Australian would have made an analogy based more on his individual experience—and on common experiences familiar to others in places of British influence—than an understanding common to this context. At that point, either he would have to explain his analogy or his listeners would have to bring in wider experience and context to compensate for the centrifugal tension.

Not only is meaning made in context, it is made through response. As we are writing this, we are responding to each other and Bakhtin overtly, even as we respond to other experiences more tacitly (Polanyi, 2009). As you are reading, you are responding as well—perhaps nodding in agreement, rolling your eyes, highlighting in turquoise, or wishing we'd get on with it already. Nevertheless, you are responding and, through your response, meaning—tentative, fragile, exploratory, formative—is being made. Bakhtin (1981) argued that you can't help but respond, that people are always responding. At least to us, the implication of that constant response is that people remain, to some extent and purpose, in dialogue.

If such is the case, then all of us and the cultures we construct remain constantly in dialogue. Note that we didn't write "perfect dialogue" or "complete dialogue." Not all dialogue, perhaps not most dialogue, feels as dialogical as we would have it be, if we interpret dialogue as recognizing a range of perspectives, and proceeding toward mutually satisfying and forward looking, but not necessarily consensual or even arrived at ends. Meaning may be made that runs counter to our existing beliefs, may cause those belief systems to wobble or even shatter into shards that cannot not be reassembled, at least not as they were. Yet, even as a series of utterances skews more toward the monological end of the continuum, there remain traces of dialogue within.

It is from this dialogical stance that we argue that people in their lived experiences transact in an ongoing dialogue of cultures. This is a conception we will continue to expand and deepen as we wend our way through this and other chapters. As we discuss the plurality of cultures, we will also explore the idea that, to an extent, people have options regarding their cultural alignments, even those like gender and race that, to many people, might not seem to offer options. It is clear, then, that we are considering what is entailed in understanding cultures and selves as in flux and in dialogue. We are also testing the limits of romantic versions of self and cultures that prize essentialism and are testing the limits of nihilistic versions of self that see plurality as chaotic, fractured, and pointless.

In considering the plurality of cultures, we continue to unpack the idea of a multivoiced, dialogical self and consider the many ways we dialogue with cultures internally and externally. We begin by exploring ideas about positioning presented by Canadian philosopher Ian Hacking. We then use numerous examples to illustrate the complexity of dialoguing across multiple external and internal cultural positions in order to raise this complexity to the surface. Realizing that such a discussion can also raise feelings of apprehension and uncertainty, we next focus on the importance of dialoguing through these concerns. Our intent across the chapter is to create some interesting places to name and think about what we do with uncertainty and difference and how, through dialogue, we can gain direction in an increasingly pluralistic and connected, but complex world. Finally, as we will throughout the book, we prompt imaginings about the ways such ideas transact with the ways you continue to learn, live, and evolve.

Constructing a Self

Connie's brief transaction reveals a dialogue *within* a multivoiced self and points to a dialogue *among* individuals, groups, institutions, and cultures. In an instance like that, when a person acts and interacts in a particular context, that person is recognized— by the self and by others—as acting and interacting as a certain "kind of person" (Hacking, 2007, p. 285) or even, as is illustrated in Connie's case, several different "kinds" at once. In that same Bahktinian way that we create shared meanings of a given word—meanings that are at once unified and, therefore, recognizable, and also variant—we also construct shared meanings of particular ways of being in the world, ways of being certain "kinds" of people (Hacking, 2007, p. 285).

INTERACTIONS AND TRANSACTIONS

In this sidebar, we unpack our differences around *interactions* and *transactions*. We hope that making visible our dialogue about these differences also reveals and operationalizes a theory of language underneath a commitment to dialogical selves. As you saw in the first sidebar, using the same word—the same set of alphabetic symbols on a page, the same set of audible sounds— does not guarantee *shared* meaning or experience. And yet, we must use symbols with each other to make sense of the world and to take action together. This is both beautiful and, at times, vexing, in part because the ways we understand, experience, value, and operationalize the same symbols—like working theory, democracy, home, immigrant, police, interaction—also creates a middling ground. However, when we act on the ideas, experiences, and perspectives—the realities and worlds—that arrive through language, we sometimes act in ways that treat our realities as *the Reality*—as something fixed, apparent, and universal. That is, as something that either *is* shared or *should be* shared.

But this view of language effectively shuts down dialogue within the self and with others; instead, this view of language either seeks to make what is obvious clear to others who should already see what is obvious, or it seeks to bring around those whose views and values are somehow inferior. In this book, we hope to rival this view of language and instead to show language to be semiotic, contextual, in flux; in these sidebars, we also hope to show that seeing language this way has profound implications for selves in dialogue and in flux and especially for possible stances toward the multiple worlds and selves created through discourse.

Framing the Dialogue (Bob)

So many of these discussions came about as we both were scouring through incomplete drafts searching on our end for a way to pick up the thread of the writing. This dialogue is no different as it begins with me writing a margin comment after wondering if I should keep changing all of Jen's *interacts* to *transacts*.

Bob: Would prefer just using *transacts* à la Rosenblatt rather than *interacts*, which for me is too two-dimensional.

Jen: Oh, interesting. I have a hard time with transacts, but I come to Rosenblatt later than you do. My guess is you've internalized a sense of that word more than I have. In fact, until you tell me, it doesn't even occur to me to use *transacts*. I also think I feel like *transacts* is implied in *interacts*. I do think this is where our tensions emerge – your lean toward dialogism and my lean toward pragmatism, even though we each value both. To me, interacts feels more internal, external, situated, inventive, and rhetorical …

Bob: OK, so maybe we need one of your beloved (smile) footnotes or maybe we create sidebars in this text where we unpack & share these discussions. We will have to, ultimately, go with one term or the other, but sharing our dialogue on that discussion might be interesting.

Jen: Actually, I like the idea of a sidebar as a convention to demonstrate dialogue with each other and with the text as we're constructing it …

Bob's Take

As I've thought about Jen's stance on these terms, I've become less insistent on a need to use one term or the other, especially knowing that Rosenblatt's use of the term *transaction* is less recognized by the public at large. Most people tend to equate the term transaction, not with mutual shaping and complexity of response, but with an exchange of money for goods or services. So, unless invoking a direct connection to the work of Rosenblatt, using either *interaction* or *transaction* may not matter to many readers.

In truth, however, I've so trained myself to separate the two terms that it's very hard for me to use interaction except in the most predictable circumstances. A good friend of mine, Jenny Oliver, who unfortunately died two years ago, used to say in her distinctly southern way, "Bob Fecho, you're about to remind us that we're transacting, aren't you?" At this point, I'm so hardwired to transact that if you see *interaction* anywhere in this text, it's a safe assumption Jen wrote it.

Jen's Take

As I've come to see the ways that Bob cares about Rosenblatt's concept of *transaction*, I've tried to use it in places where I might otherwise use *interaction*. I also went back to Rosenblatt's text to see which scholars she was drawing on, and I've begun reading John Dewey and Arthur Bentley's book, *The Knowing and the Known*—the scholarship that largely informed her work on transactions.

As a rhetorician and a pragmatist, there are concepts and values that I try to hold for in writing this book with Bob. There is a lot of thinking between Bob and me that resonates, but occasionally we diverge, and when something in the text causes me to pause, I try to listen for what values are underneath what Bob is articulating and what histories inform his stance. I ask myself, "What's he up to right here?" and with particular regard to ways our thinking diverges, "What's the difference that makes a difference here?" In this case, our dialogue about *transactions* and *interactions* raised more questions and also reconnected me to John Dewey, a pragmatist. So, I find myself wanting to listen in on the dialogue among Dewey, Bentley, and Rosenblatt for the light that dialogue will shine on my next steps.

And perhaps as a side note to the sidebar, even these moves to be in dialogue with Bob in this way are born out of dialogue, an inquiry stance, and a practice of descriptive review that I learned through another text I often use with young people and with teachers: "Starting with what is: Exploring response and responsibility to student writing through collaborative inquiry" (Simon, 2013).

Being recognized as a certain "kind of person" in a given context is connected to identity, something we'll discuss more in Chapter 4, and connected to cultures and the ways we come to share recognitions, a concept we'll unpack a bit in this chapter. Here we will continue to layer onto Nieto's and Said's conceptions of cultures, this time calling on the work of Ian Hacking and James Gee, in order to discuss the ways cultures and the dialogical self interact in and across contexts.

Hacking (2007) described two important phenomena related to the ways we come to recognize a person as a particular kind of person: "making up people" and the "looping effect." Hacking explained, "'making up people,' referred to the ways in which a new scientific classification may bring into being a new kind of person, conceived of and experienced as a new way to be a person" (p. 285). Let's think about Connie's identity as a teacher consultant (TC) for her local National Writing Project (NWP) site. After all, being a TC is a relatively new "kind of person" (Hacking, 2007, p. 285) to be.

In 1974, in a grassroots effort to put "teachers at the center," James Gray (2000) convened the inaugural summer institute of the Bay Area Writing Project—the first of its kind in the country—and worked with two dozen teachers to create a model of professional development that promoted teachers sharing with teachers. This effort was in large part a response to discontent with ways of being a writing teacher at the time, ways often constrained by institutions and ways that likely still echo for many writing teachers now: working in isolation to other colleagues, feeling pressure over growing public concern about young people's writing abilities, participating in mandated top-down professional development that was often less than helpful.

During that first summer institute, writing teachers wrote with and for each other, offered demonstrations of their own teaching, and discussed ways of adapting others' approaches for their own students, although none of these were yet requirements of the institute. In the following years, summer institute participants tried to cultivate partnerships with local schools to offer more teacher-centered professional development. Several of their efforts bombed, but they finally landed on one that worked. As these teacher leaders headed into subsequent summer institutes, an endeavor they were now quite committed to, they evolved particular practices for teachers participating in summer institutes and they began to enact particular models for in-service professional development.

Yet, even though the term *model* was frequently used as NWP developed—a term that implies a certain concretizing for many who hear it—those practices remained in dialogue across the numerous local sites of the organization. One result of this dialogue is that if observers visit a number of those local sites, they will see practices that look similar to what was seen in other sites, but have a distinct local spin and interpretation brought to them. Visitors would also no doubt see practices that are peculiar to the existence of that site alone. Therefore, teachers who take part in NWP summer institutes have some shared understanding of that experience that allows them to, at the annual meeting, engage with teachers from across the country and wildly diverse backgrounds as if they taught next to each other in the same school. Simultaneously, however, those dialogues also unpack the many interpretations of NWP culture that exist across the nearly 200 local sites and the thousands of allied teachers.

To distinguish an NWP writing teacher as a different kind of teacher, the NWP created the term and role of *teacher consultant*. For the NWP, teacher consultants are the kinds of writing teachers who write, who share their writing with students and teachers, who share their practices with other teachers, and who seek to be leaders in their schools and communities, inviting other teachers to write and learn alongside them. After completing the summer institute, these TCs attended follow-up meetings during the school year to stay in touch with fellow NWP teacher consultants and to further their own writing and learning with other teachers. These TCs also were often invited to lead in-service workshops in their schools and to co-facilitate subsequent summer institutes, which is the conversation Bob and Connie are having at the start of this chapter.

After participating in a summer institute, a teacher like Connie would be recognized as a teacher consultant and called a teacher consultant by the National

Writing Project, but might not yet recognize herself as, in writing project parlance, a TC. Over time, let's say she participates in the shared practices of the writing project—writing with other teachers, speaking at conferences, leading in-service professional development, co-facilitating other summer writing projects. As she does these things—and even if she doesn't—an internal dialogue is taking place between the ways she recognizes other TCs and the way she recognizes herself as a TC. If she participates in these practices and recognizes some resonance between what she's doing, as well as how and why, and what, how, and why other TCs are doing, then over time she will likely come to recognize herself as a particular kind of person: an NWP teacher consultant.

For Connie and thousands of teachers across the United States, the National Writing Project created a new way to be a teacher. That is to say, they created both a culture and potential I-position for a teacher to experience. This is what Hacking calls "making up a person" (p. 285). To summarize Hacking: Previously, X was not a way to be a person; people did not experience themselves in this way. They did not interact with their colleagues, their students, their families, their employers, their counselors in this way. Over time, this became a way to be a person, to experience oneself, to live in society (p. 299). This is true for Connie and other teacher consultants; this is also true for people who have come to see themselves as gamers, hackers, snowboarders, autistic, obese, or disrupters, among other relatively new ways of being.

A second equally important phenomenon that Hacking noted is "the looping effect." The language people give to their experiences of the world, when recognized by others, creates and lends some stability to the cultures they participate in and to the potential I-positions they may take on. Sometimes the names given to these ways of being in the world can seem to take on a life of their own as we come to think of certain kinds of people—people with ADHD or people who are gay or atheist or hunters or Latino/a or teacher consultants—as given, as definite groups or types defined by definite characteristics.

And yet, thankfully, we and the ways we recognize ourselves and others are far more fluid than that, changing dynamically within and across transactions. People sometimes revolt against the ways others have recognized and named them, "enhanc[ing] and adjust[ing] what is true of them" and "changing conceptions of who the people are, both for 'us' and for 'them'" (Hacking, 2007, p. 289). These changed conceptions "loop" back around to "upgrade self-conceptions and raise consciousness" (Hacking 2007, p. 290). There is, thus, a sense in which our ways of being and the language we give to those experiences are "moving targets" (Hacking, 2007, p. 293). That movement—sometimes made explicit and visible in a particular context and sometimes bubbling just under the surface and sometimes faintly stirring in nearly unobservable ways—points to multicultural selves in dialogue with multiple cultures and the unifying, dis-unifying ways those cultures are performed and created in the transactions among multicultural selves.

Dialoguing with Multiple Cultures

Of course, the ways people recognize themselves and others and the ways they "loop back" to alter those recognitions are always performed in highly situated ways. The "kind of person" someone is recognized as "being" in a particular time and place can change from moment to moment with something as simple as an uttered word or a tossed gesture or a subtle environmental change, and how a person is recognized can change from one situation to the next, and of course, can be ambiguous and unstable (Gee, 2000, p. 1). For dimmed lighting or fingers held and separated into the "Live Long and Prosper" V of Star Trek fans to *signify* a way of being, the meaning of the *symbol* must in some way be shared in order to be recognized.

These recognitions occur through the processes of "making up people" and "looping back," where recognitions are sometimes enthusiastically constructed and received, sometimes tensely negotiated, and sometimes seen and marked but not valued or accepted. Part of what it means to become a certain "kind of person" is that you share in the practices and symbols that signify what it means to you and others to be that "kind of person" *and* that you to some degree share also in the meaning and valuing of those symbols and practices. I-positions are created, shaped, sustained, and remade through dialogic transactions with people and materials that carry and perform the symbols, recognitions, meanings, and values of multiple cultures.

Some I-positions individuals have some say in and control over; as Gee (2003) notes, a person can, to some degree, make decisions to become a college professor or a Trekkie. Others, like being a twin, have nothing to do with a person's choice; those I-positions rely on a state of being, on biology (Gee, 2003). And yet, a twin will not experience himself as a twin unless there is some shared sense of what it means to be a twin. That is, "[I-positions] only become [I-positions] because they are *recognized*" (Gee, 2000, p. 3) by the self or others as somehow meaningful in the sense that they constitute (at least in part and for now) the kind of person someone sees themselves as being.

There are plenty of biological traits that people possess that are not recognized as ways of being a kind of person. To follow Gee's example, people have spleens but, for the time being at least, that doesn't necessarily constitute anything meaningful for us or for you about being a kind of person. I-positions gain recognition and force through the workings of historical, institutional, and sociocultural forces. Even so, none of us are strictly bound by these forces. Some of us may be more bound by these forces than others. Some of us may know, to some degree, the ways we are bound and others of us may be unaware or less aware. Some of us may be more and differently harmed by the ways we are bound than others. Some of us may face grave costs for resisting the ways these forces bind us. These forces have sway as they structure and sequence recognizable ways of showing up. Over time, the familiarity of these forces comes to create norms of respect or civility or decorum, norms that become commonplaces informing not only ways of being and ways of relating but also the moralities underneath them.

A person's participation in historically and institutionally recognized ways of being often occurs in mundane, everyday decisions—like what to wear to school—that over time become routinized and the codes they carry, invisible. As you'll see later in this chapter, when there is some disruption in patterned, routine, habitual ways of participating, the patterned participation itself (i.e., what a boy can wear), what the pattern signals about being a certain kind of person (in this case, being a boy), and the kinds of people available to be, are all revealed as dialogic choices—risky, contested, costly choices perhaps, but choices nonetheless.

We offer that all cultural affiliations require a certain degree of participation on the part of individuals, even affiliations that appear deeply rooted in biology or long acknowledged social constructions. For example, the seemingly pervasive concept of gender—of masculine and feminine—is a social construct and based to a great extent on visible physical attributes of sex (male/female), and basic functions that, at one stage of evolution in some cultural groups, were more clearly proscribed to one sex or another. In blunt terms, in some cultures, men hunted, women foraged; men protected, women nurtured; men explored, women kept the fire.

With survival being the catalyst, clear demarcations and simple classifications pervaded, differences shaped by historical differences in agricultural systems (Alesina, Giuliano, & Nunn, 2011). In some cultures, hunting, protecting, exploring came to mean masculine; foraging, nurturing, keeping fire came to mean feminine. As agricultural systems developed, other gender norms emerged around plough agriculture and hoe agriculture, norms that persisted and are still reflected in gendered participation in the workplace, in politics, and in entrepreneurial activities (Alesina, Giuliano, & Nunn, 2011). Thus, in some cultures, bodies with certain biological features signified certain kinds of roles. Over time as technologies changed, men had an advantage in their historical knowledge of farming, and gendered specializations persisted despite the fact that technologies, like animal ploughs, would have permitted a shift in roles. This division of labor then generated norms about the accepted roles of women in society (Alesina, Giuliano, & Nunn, 2011).

However, it is worth noting that by marking some groups' shared meanings of a sign—i.e., sex (male/female) meant gendered roles (masculine/feminine)—we are not saying that those features *caused* gender. People then performed, and now perform, being men and women as well as gender neutral and gender fluid, differently in different contexts no matter what biological features were part of their bodies.

There is also a long history of multiple genders among ancient and contemporary societies. Within Native American communities (Lang, 1998; Nanda, 2011), such extensions of the notion of gender beyond a construct of two often have been connected to the shamans or mystics of the tribe. Such gender variation, rather than being seen as deviant or marginal, is instead viewed by most Native American and non-Native American anthropologists—and Native people themselves—as "a normative part of the [Native American] sex/gender system" (Nanda, 2011, p. 48). Similarly, hijras in India also represent a liminal state—a gender of transition—frequently associated with spirituality (Lai, 1999; Nanda, 1994). As these examples demonstrate, concepts of gender beyond strictly masculine and feminine classifications are not necessarily new and have existed for centuries.

Despite evidence in some cultures of conceiving gender as multiple and fluid rather than dual and fixed, the concept of two genders has dominated modern Western society. But the complex relationships of those of us living in technological and globalized existences have created contexts that not only allow, but may even necessitate rethinking how much of the world's population looks at gender. Certainly most of us within easy access of digital communication are aware that our neighborhood has increased to global proportions. The concerns of a lesbian couple who have adopted a daughter, the anxiety of a face-veiled Muslim woman given extra scrutiny as she navigates the aisles of a crowded mall, and the complications of ultra-Orthodox Jews as they try to maintain the gender restrictions of their faith on an airplane, even if not experienced first-hand, are frequently brought into our lives via social media and digital communication. Individuals living in such complexity often feel given to relate to those contexts in more, well, complex ways with a greater acknowledgement of the intricacies of such complexity.

So what has in the past and still remains for many to be two clear-cut classifications may for others hold nuances that provide opportunity to conceive of a range of classifications, or subclassifications at the very least. Dividing all humans simply into male and female and associating particular roles and practices with particular bodies may have outlived its usefulness as societies around the world move forward into continued global transactions. Certainly we know of many adults and adolescents—and even young children—who question the sex (male/female) that signifies gendered roles, despite the genitalia present on their bodies.

Although mainstream society may position all of us into male or female slots based solely on traditional standards of classification, a growing minority of people push back on those classifications. They argue and insist that they are not as mainstream culture has dictated, but are the other as they see themselves, the preferred. Some scholars, like Judith Butler, have argued that gender (masculine/feminine) is not an identity at all but a performance, and a performance that is not necessarily connected to a person's sex (male/female). Gender is what you *do*, not who you are. Butler contended that we all put on a gender performance, regardless of whether we choose to do that in ways that are culturally traditional or not. The question then, is not whether or not we will perform gender, but *how* we will perform it.

The point of this discussion isn't necessarily to make the case for multiple sexes or multiple genders—although we think such a construction is worth developing—but instead is to introduce the belief that all cultures and the I-positions these

Butler - "how" we perform gender

cultures construct and allow, in the end, require a certain degree of participation on the part of those positioned within them. We are in no way denying that powerful forces of compliance and conformity collude, for example, to have individuals accept racial and gender designations. Equally, we are well aware that people falling into the shade of Alzheimer's or some other debilitating mental disease lose a great deal of agency in terms of how they construct the cultures they enter. However, we argue that, to varying degrees, such designations must be embraced, accepted, or tolerated by whomever society affixes them to in order to remain viable and in place.

The designations of male and White can be thrust upon someone, but they, just as we opted for the gender-ambiguous singular *they*, can think, feel, and act otherwise. Consider, for example, two youths—Jared, a gay boy, and Pascale, a lesbian—who decide to run for homecoming court during their senior year. They tell their friends over Facebook and Twitter that they will dress in drag for homecoming if their friends will nominate them to the homecoming court. Students across the school rally and the two are nominated. The administrators of this historically conservative school in the southwest hear that the youth plan to show up in drag, and call Jared and Pascale to the office individually. The vice principal is disturbed by what seems a clear disruption of tradition. The principal is worried about backlash from Mormon parents. A gay faculty advisor for student council tells the queer youths that since gay people have just won the right to get married in the state, the worry is that people will see these youths as "roaches coming out of the woodwork." All three faculty members agree that their concern is with Jared dressing in drag; they are not concerned about Pascale.

In this situation, the longstanding, male, football-oriented tradition of homecoming is recognized by administrators—and, they imagine, by particular kinds of alumni—through certain features that, over time, celebrate and construct a shared understanding of what it means to "come home" to this particular high school. Like many high schools across the country, this school marks the phenomena of "coming home" by institutional events and practices including pep rallies where football players and cheerleaders perform, a student election for homecoming court, tailgating at the homecoming football game played against a lesser opponent, a half-time showcase of the homecoming court in formal attire, an announcement and crowning of a king and queen, and a postgame dance to celebrate a glorious football win and newly crowned "royalty."

These practices create recognizable ways of being football players, cheerleaders, high school students, alumni, girls, boys, men, women. However, when a person like Jared or Pascale—or Sam, their female-to-male transgender friend—disrupts or rewrites a practice, a moment of wobble is created for all directly involved and all indirectly witnessing. In the ensuing uncertainty, the practices by which certain kinds of people are recognized and valued—and others not—are also rewritten. It becomes clear that the dialogue occurring is not merely internal nor simply interpersonal when it is externalized; rather, the dialogue is also with the

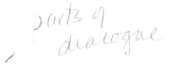

people, symbols, meanings, values, and practices that are historical, institutional, and sociocultural.

In their homecoming bid, Jared and Pascale are in dialogue with many cultures at once—through the ways they and others in the room are performing as certain "kinds of people" and also "looping back," and through the ways they and others call to mind and bring to bear other cultures and institutions. Jared and Pascale are, then, not only dialoguing among their own multiple I-positions and accompanying cultures but also among those of their peers who nominated them, those of faculty who support and/or govern them, those of their parents, those of others who are named, remembered, and invoked in these transactions.

This also means that they are in dialogue with the multiple ways these I-positions are recognized, performed, and valued across multiple cultures. That is, Jared and Pascale are also in dialogue with the homecoming rituals of this school and many other schools; with the ways of being those rituals are meant to enact, teach, protect, and perpetuate; with the authorities and institutions that legitimize, normalize, and reproduce those ways of being. They are in dialogue with a long history of drag in ancient Roman literary arts, Native American spirituality, Chinese theater, and modern American films; with the Stonewall Riots, a pivotal civil rights moment in the LGBTQ community, reportedly led and inspired by drag queens.

They are in dialogue with the gay faculty advisor's experiences of LGBTQ culture, which seem to vary quite a bit from Jared's and Pascale's experiences of LGBTQ culture; with local derogatory ways that heterosexuals sometimes see and transact with people who are gay; with cultural ways of understanding and performing genders; with legislation related to gay marriage. They are in dialogue with the Mormon seminary across from the school where Mormon students spend part of their school day and return to campus with anti-LGBTQ pamphlets; with an after-school group Jared and Pascale attended that supports LGBTQ youth; and with many other institutions, affinity groups, and local publics that were not named in the meeting but nevertheless were shaping internal and external transactions in the moment.

In these transactions, from moment to moment, Jared and Pascale—and the others in the room—are experiencing different degrees of tension and solidarity with cultures that have shaped and, in some cases, given rise to, their available I-positions. We certainly want to highlight the fact that these cultural dialogues are occurring. We also want to highlight that seeing ourselves and others as selves-in-dialogue with multiple cultures opens up a range of possibilities regarding cultural alignments and invites us to consider, in a given moment, how we might determine more precise ways of pursuing desire (Tuck, 2009) and justice in a given transaction.

This seems especially important to recognize and think about in institutions like schools that serve a socializing role for youth through the day-to-day schedule, class routines, celebration of holidays and school events, literatures and *schools create a constrain available "I positions."*

histories included and excluded, pedagogical practices, dress codes, standardized assessments, and the like. Institutions, like aesthetic forms, reveal and reproduce what we believe about ourselves and others, about the kinds of people it is okay—or not okay—to be. Institutions, like schools, help to create or constrain available I-positions by what they will or won't recognize, by what cultural practices they condone or ban. As Said noted with regard to literature, with institutions, too, there is often an elevating element—sometimes traditions, like homecoming—that carries culture and reproduces certain kinds of selves and yet is thought to be above the fray, untouchable, unable to be looped back.

Connecting to Practice

The young people who come into our classrooms—all of us, really—are multicultural meaning makers interpreting, negotiating, and constructing ideas and practices, materials and relationships, limits and possibilities with others. In these Connecting to Practice sections, we hope to imagine with you possibilities for supporting the multi-literacies and dialogical selves of these young people we care about by constructing the classroom as a space of inquiry and dialogue attuned to the complexity and uncertainty young people are navigating internally and externally across multicultural contexts and communities. Rather than offering activities or practices, instead we offer approaches and strategies for creating a rich context in which individual and collaborative meaning making might mutually fuel one another.

Constructing a shared and sustained dialogue

To create a shared dialogue is to create a compelling reason for young people to read and write, listen and learn, design and deliberate together. Creating a sustained dialogue means that shared meaning making is extended over time and across texts, increases in complexity over time, and is responsive to the connections and questions that emerge along the way. Overarching, existentially perplexing questions with no easy answers help students connect their work in class and support possibilities for exploring a multivoiced self. What does it mean to "grow up"? How do individuals and communities negotiate conflict? What makes for meaningful work? What responsibilities should individuals and communities have toward each other? How do people construct a moral code for themselves? Questions such as these invite students to engage in dialogues that have fascinated people for ages, to connect their lives to academic contexts, and to see reading and writing as meaning-making activities rather than merely work assigned.

Valuing multiple perspectives

To invite young people into considering and responding to a range of possible perspectives—from those perhaps most familiar to those least familiar—you might

material

include poems, short stories, TED talks, documentaries, audio essays, songs, editorials, academic articles, newspaper blogs, and so on that demonstrate a range of thinking that overlaps, contradicts, raises questions, surprises, and complicates students' (and your) ideas. Juxtaposing, mapping, dramatizing these in relation to one another and unpacking what's at stake in these perspectives—the differences that make a difference—can begin to reveal a complex dialogue already in motion and can set the stage for students' unpacking their own inner dialogues in relation to the ideas they're brushing up against in class through texts and with their peers.

Exploring a multivoiced self

Hacking's 2 Concepts

To connect to their own lives and to make sense of their selves-in-dialogue, students might take into account Hacking's two concepts—"making up a person" and the "looping effect"—in relation to an overarching question and the complexities emerging in texts and in conversation. By way of example, consider possibilities for this question: How do people construct a moral code for themselves? Students might first consider the ways different cultural communities they are part of teach or value or enforce or invite a certain kind of moral code in the ways they teach or discipline or enforce or invite people to be a certain kind of moral person. Young people might consider, What is the kind of moral person my cultures and communities—my church or synagogue or mosque, my school, my soccer team, my online artist group, my World of Warcraft friends, my family— would have me be? They might also consider what they experience as shared and distinct as well as at odds and in tension—maybe not all the time, but in certain situations or under certain conditions—across the ways each of those cultures would shape a moral person. And how do they find themselves "looping back" or wanting to loop back to resist or reshape their own way of being a moral person as well as the ways each community teaches or disciplines or enforces or invites a certain way of being a moral person? Where do they feel most sure and most uncertain about the moral codes of these communities and about their own developing moral code?

Richly situating dialogical selves

The ways young people respond to questions like these—in classrooms and in their lived lives—are not abstract, nor are they universal. Neither are the multiliteracies needed for navigating multicultural contexts and dialogical selves isolated school-based textual practices far removed from the complex situations in which young people find themselves. Instead, young people need ways of learning to theorize *in situ* and of learning to leverage their multiple literacies to negotiate and transform possibilities as they loop back on the selves their cultures and communities would construct for them. Toward this end, students need opportunities to create and discuss texts, broadly construed, that situate and reimagine their

yes

dialogical selves in real time as they experience pressures and pulls to be different kinds of moral people in a single moment.

Institutions often study or support or count or educate or evaluate people who have been recognized as a "kind of person," creating knowledge, including assumptions and presumptions that are "taught, disseminated, refined and applied with the context of institutions" (Hacking, 2007, p. 297). The knowledge that is created and circulated—knowledge that may change over time or may later be debunked—is constructed by professionals, experts who come to know or be seen to know about certain "kinds of people" and by the people themselves, who possess their own kind of expertise. It is often the institutional *experts* who:

> generate or legitimate knowledge … judge its validity, and use it in their practice. They work within … institutions that guarantee their legitimacy, authenticity, and status as experts. They study, try to help, or advise on the control of, the people who are classified as a given kind.
>
> *(Hacking, 2007, p. 297).*

This phenomenon holds for institutional I-positions, like teacher consultant, and also for other kinds of I-positions like being an identical twin, a charismatic person, or a "Trekkie" (Gee, 2000, p. 3). We come to know and construct our I-positions and others' I-positions—as an introvert, as autistic, as middle-class, as cisgender, as a nurse, as a photographer—through the language and signs we give to these classifications. Likewise, such construction occurs through the groups, practices, knowledge, experts, and expertise, and the institutions we form and change because of and through the language and signs we leverage to make sense of and perform and resist what it means to be certain "kinds of people." In a given moment in a particular time and place, there is a way in which a given I-position is in dialogue with all the groups, practices, knowledge, experts and expertise, institutions, language and signs that, up to that moment, have given shape to the self's unifying and individualizing understandings of what it means to be that "kind of person" (Hacking, 2007, p 197).

Dialoguing through Uncertainty

At this point, we invite you to attend to and embrace any sense of wobble you're experiencing with the scenarios and concepts we've been outlining. We feel a sense of wobble ourselves as we make meaning of these complexities in this text and in our own lives. We don't want you to get bogged down in the complexities of the cultural dialoguing that is always going on within and among dialogical selves. We would, however, like you to consider that the transactions between individuals and the cultures in which they participate are most likely either more complex than you thought or, at least, more complex than you've been willing to admit to and work within. All that to the good, we don't want you feeling so overwhelmed by complexity and uncertainty that it paralyzes you or gets you seeking what Hermans and Hermans-Konopka (2010) have called a search for pre-dialogical certainty. Instead, in this chapter and in this book, we're trying to urge you to add ways to seek a more stable *post*-dialogical understanding.

Most of us, at various times in our lives, attempt to create certainty out of uncertainty. Sometimes we try to do this by limiting the range of positions and voices in our lives; consider the friend who suddenly stops participating in social media or a co-worker who quits a high-paying but high-stress job to become a librarian in a rural county. Another tack is to award dominance to one position, either an interior or exterior one. Supporters of extreme and often unexamined political views might fall under this umbrella. A third approach is to make bound- aries between self and others stark or of high contrast, from whence xenophobia arises, or from whence come campaigns to keep others (i.e., anyone who isn't us, whatever that us may be) in a position of subservience. Lastly and paradoxically, by adding in a new position, people can hope for achieving certainty in order to find solace through that new position. Someone who leaps into a new profession or seeks in a new partner what was lacking in a former partner is on a quest for certainty through addition (Hermans & Hermans-Konopka, 2010). These tacks are all quests for pre-dialogical certainty—*pre*-dialogical because of the ways they seek to gain certainty before, and often instead of, being in dialogue with the uncertainty that has arisen.

Our aim at this point is for you to consider a fifth approach, one that, much like turning into a skid on an icy road, may at first feel counterintuitive. Similarly, when confronted with uncertainty within a moment of wobble, we encourage you to turn into uncertainty rather than steering to avoid it. As such, dialogue becomes its own process for negotiating the uncertainty involved with the wobble created by dialogue. By dialoguing with others and/or oneself around an issue that has created a sense of uncertainty, individuals enter into an open-ended and flexible process that has no predetermined destination or outcome. Instead, all parties and positions are openly invited to contribute toward a mutually constructed end that, if not creating certainty, reduces uncertainty (Hermans & Hermans-Konopka, 2010). What can at first feel full of dread can morph into a space rife with possibility.

One point of departure we have/had with these ideas posited by Hermans and Hermans-Konopka (2010) is their use of the term *post-dialogical* certainty when discussing the use of dialogue, as they indicate, to "travel into uncertainty" (p. 47). Based on ideas by David Snowden and Mary Boone (2007), we wonder if com- plexity ever yields certainty or solutions. This is not to say that we cannot address concerns or difficulties in meaningful ways or that we throw our hands up or are let off the hook by complex social problems simply because they are complex and can't be "solved." Instead, we are recognizing the limited nature of knowledge, of perspectives, of experiences as well as the ways we are all bound by time and space and context and, yet, need to be able to get things done even when a course of action is necessary and less than ideal and when outcomes are unpredictable.

As a friend says, people traffic in contingency, in the unforeseen and the unpredictable. Our decisions, understandings, and actions, then, are always revisable, always responsive to new data, to the back talk of a situation. A decision or a given course of action, no matter how longstanding, is tenuous, tentative, limited, changeable, and rarely, if ever, ultimate or final. Even the best of options needs to be continually assessed, tweaked, or sometimes abandoned. Knowing this requires, to some extent, that we approach situations from a stance of inquiry and of venturing, even in situations where we have a great deal of expertise and where we feel quite strongly about the issues and the outcomes.

In Snowden and Boone's scheme, decisions get made in one of five contexts: simple, complicated, complex, chaotic, and disorderly. Simple and complicated issues—likened to threading a needle or unraveling a mass of cables respectively—are marked by straightforward cause-and-effect situations and have clear solutions. Chaotic and disorderly contexts are marked by high and even higher turbulence and render decision-making difficult and risky.

Complexity, where we believe most modern learning situations exist, is a space where "right answers can't be ferreted out" (Snowden & Boone, 2007, p. 5). They liken difference between complicated and complex contexts to differences between a Ferrari and the Brazilian rainforest. Although complicated, a Ferrari can be disassembled and put back together in working order by a trained mechanic. On the other hand, the issues of the Brazilian rainforest involve such a range of dynamic variables that right answers and permanent solutions are at best elusive, if ever achieved. Snowden and Boone's comparison holds, if we consider the difference between creating or building a structure where we can reliably see whether or not a thing—a bridge, a car, a tower—has been built and fixing or repairing where we cannot always reliably diagnose or achieve our aim—as in medicine or mechanics—and where we often have to make decisions under constraints of time, money, and our own limited expertise. In complex situations, we cannot reliably bring about what we aim for.

Teachers, business executives, parents, politicians, and anyone else operating within complexity, need to look for patterns and trends in order to discern possible paths in which to move forward. In the global and technological complexity of the world we're constructing, the only certainty is that, at least to some extent, uncertainty will remain, urging us toward greater and more extensive dialogue.

Many of us who teach do so in contexts where administrations and regulatory agencies want to manage complexity, as if they actually could. Paced and standardized curriculums, along with standardized tests, are attempts by administrators and policymakers to impose simple or at most complicated solution-oriented practices into complex, solution-resistant situations. Teaching literature interpretation through the YA novel *Out of the Pocket* is, as we indicated in our Introduction, a complex activity when dealing with a single student and the range of cultural I-positions that student brings to the work. Now multiply that complexity by 30 or 150 students and even in a racially or gender homogenous school the spectrum and fluidity of cultural response is huge.

Moving Forward

The point here is not to try to manage complexity nor to throw up your hands and ignore it. Instead, the idea is to wade into that complexity with all its inherent uncertainty and imagine the dialogical learning opportunities presented. It is useless to try to be an expert on the many cultures in your classroom; they are too many and too dynamic. Instead, you need to become an expert of inquiring into and dialogically engaging with the rich networks and knots that emerge as those cultures connect and tangle with each other. We argue that it is incumbent on all of us who educate ourselves and others to help our students inquire into and dialogue with complexity if we are to prepare them at all for the unpredictable and intertwined contexts they will face as they enter adulthood.

To this point, we've been mostly sketching the theoretical landscape of the ideas that will underpin the remainder of our discussion, particularly as all of these issues relate to education in general and literacy education in particular. What, we ask, does the considering of multiple cultures and multiple I-positions mean for teaching and learning with adolescents? In doing so, we've laid a foundation based on the ways language is constantly pulled centrally toward unification and away from center toward greater individualization. It is within such tension-filled contexts that learning occurs and meaning is constructed. It is also within such fluidity that people make new ways of being and, in pushing against how they've been slotted or labeled by others, loop around to upgraded conceptions of self. By calling traditional notions of gender into question and introducing other ways of considering what we mean by that term, we've invited you to experience a sense of wobble that might open you to more complex, but also more nuanced and progressive understandings. Ultimately we've argued that rather than avoiding complexity and the uncertainty that often accompanies it, all educators need to find ways to dialogue through the uncertainty into a post-dialogical space. The next chapter, focused on how cultures and the dialogical self transact with learning, will help us all move toward that end. But we promise no solution; just useful paths to consider.

References

Alesina, A., Giuliano, P., and Nunn, N. (2011). On the origins of gender roles: Women and the plough. *The Quarterly Journal of Economics* 128(2), 469–530.

Bakhtin, M. (1981). *The dialogic imagination: Four essays by M. M. Bakhtin*. C. Emerson and M. Holquist, Trans. Austin, TX: U of Texas Press. (Original work published 1975.)

Bakhtin, M. (1986). *Speech genres & other late essays*. V. W. McGee, Trans. Austin, TX: U of Texas Press.

Freire, P. (1970). *Pedagogy of the oppressed*. Myra Bergman Ramos, Trans. New York: Continuum Publishing Company.

Gee, J. (2000). Identity as an analytic lens for research in education. *Review of Research in Education* 25, 99–125.

Gray, J. (2000). *Teachers at the center: A memoir of the early years of the National Writing Project*. Berkeley, CA: National Writing Project Press.

Hacking, I. (2007). Kinds of people: Moving targets. *British Academy Lecture* 11 April 2006.

Hermans, H. and Hermans-Konopka, A. (2010). *Dialogical self theory: Positioning and counter-positioning in a globalizing society*. Cambridge: Cambridge UP.

Lai, V. (1999). Not this, not that: The Hijras of India and the cultural politics of sexuality. *Social Text* 17(4), 119–140.

Lang, S. (1998). *Men as women, women as men: Changing gender in Native American cultures*. Austin, TX: U of Texas Press.

Nanda, S. (1994). *Hijras*. Hoboken, NJ: Wiley.

Nanda, S. (2011). *Gender diversity: Crosscultural variations*. Long Grove, IL: Waveland Press.

Polanyi, M. (2009). *The tacit dimension*. Chicago, IL: University of Chicago Press.

Simon, R. (2013). Starting with what is: Exploring response and responsibility to student writing through collaborative inquiry. *English Education* 45(2), 115–146.

Snowden, D. and Boone, M. (2007). A leader's framework for decision-making. *Harvard Business Review: The essential guide to leadership* (pp. 59–68).

Tuck, E. (2009). Suspending damage: An open letter to communities. *Harvard Educational Review* 79(3), 409–427.

2

LEARNING, CULTURES, AND THE DIALOGICAL SELF

"So here I was trying to start this literature lesson that was being observed by district personnel, and all every student who was entering my classroom would talk about was the big fight that had just happened in the cafeteria."

The speaker is Cassie, a first-year teacher at a comprehensive high school in a small city in the US South. Her mix of African American, Latino/a, and White high school students had been seemingly supercharged by the cafeteria eruption. They were animated, to say the least, sparking colorful descriptions of what had gone down, offering causes and results, and generally unpacking the event and the possible upshots.

In the meantime, Cassie was well aware that she had a literature lesson that needed teaching. Her rising anxiety was only complicated by the district personnel who had come to observe her and try out a new observation checklist in the process. Although no one said anything outright, she could sense a growing impatience among the visitors, and she felt tugged to do the teacher thing, put an end to the hubbub, and get on with the lesson.

On the other hand, Cassie was also well aware of the energy that was percolating in the room, that is, the engaged energy emanating from the tales being told by the adolescents. They were boisterous, talking over one another, colorfully piling detail upon contradiction upon exclamation. It was wrong, she thought, to just clamp down on all this excitement, suck the air from the room, and abruptly shift. Yet, it was also wrong to not use the moment and all that energy to some co-constructed, positive end. If a person could become the flag in the middle of a tug-of-war, Cassie could tell you first-hand what it would feel like.

If you teach, you've found yourself in a similar context: stretched between the need to bring some unity to whatever was occurring in the classroom and the desire to explore and engage the many paths and perspectives offered by the range of individuals involved. It's as if you're simultaneously thinking, "How do I end this?" and "How do I keep it going?" You sense there's something important going on, but also sense that it could easily implode, or worse, explode, leaving the lesson or, great fear of fears, your career in shambles.

At the time, most likely neither you nor Cassie felt that you were in a sweet spot, a space conducive to learning. As we noted in Chapter 1, embracing the disequilibrium caused by wobble and working dialogically through the uncertainty feels counterintuitive. Sure, you're thinking, I'll crash and burn if I do that. Yet, skewing wholly to either side of the continuum, when you think on it, doesn't feel comforting either. Completely ignoring this large-scale disruption or just letting all the *sturm und drang* play out don't feel to be useful ways to engage students in reflective understandings of their lives.

Complicating this scenario are the overt and tacit implications of cultural values, perspectives, experiences, and ongoing meaning making that overlay and undergird the context. What meaning were the district observers making of the commotion? We know that Cassie as a young White female, inexperienced teacher, sensitive crosser of cultures, devotee of pop culture, and a wide number of other I-positions was situated in a moment of wobble. We're sure that the students were bringing a range of cultural experiences and values to the outpouring that unpacked the fight. And no doubt allegiances among the tenuous and ever-changing cohorts that often mark the stratifications—who's in and who's out; who's ascending and who's descending—of adolescent culture were being expressed and even tested. Finally, somewhere in the background of what Bakhtin (1981) might describe as a "dialogically agitated and tension filled environment of alien words, value judgments, and accents," the pervasive culture of her school and the larger culture of English teaching were weighing in on the event (p. 276).

Wading into what's been churned up among our own cultural positions can be daunting. Add the cultural positions, the artifacts of cultural production (e.g., a lesson plan, a literary text, a 50-minute class period, an upcoming test, a new administrative checklist for assessment and surveillance), the fleeting nature of these moments, and the power dynamics at play in a scenario like Cassie was facing, and it can be difficult to know how to act at all, let alone how to foster learning. Scenarios like these—rich and complex and ordinary—raise a host of questions: What counts as learning and who gets to count? What does learning look like? What in youth gets kick-started by a physical encounter? Whose values should rise to the surface, if any? Should middle-class expectations of order and decorum be imposed on all learners? Is a culture of accountability counter to a culture of generating multiple understandings?

So Where Is This Going?

Cassie, like other teachers and students we've introduced to illustrate the dialogical self in motion, found herself in dialogue with multiple voices within as well as with the multiple voices and cultures of others. Remember Connie as she weighed her options and tried to decide about co-leading the summer institute with Bob. In her case, we foregrounded an internal dialogue, even though it had been performed as a kind of think aloud. In a few situations, we've highlighted verbal dialogue with others and historical and sociocultural dynamics playing out in sometimes rather tense ways. Take, for example, the youth attempting to queer homecoming practices, much to the dismay of school administrators. Some moments have focused more on a specific interaction playing out and then zoomed out to consider the multiple transactions unfolding. Some scenarios have highlighted an informal moment between friends; others are contextualized in a more formalized classroom environment, where the risks and stakes of actions or inactions might carry different weight. In this chapter, we aim to keep the dynamism and complexity of scenes like these near and present while we also consider what it might entail to bring meaning making—textual, visual, material, mediated, performative, and so on—front and center.

Of course, these kinds of situations in which we encounter people with experiences, ideas, cultures, languages, values, and relationships quite distinct from our own are more and more common in schools, in workplaces, over the internet, down the street, and around the world. With new technologies, global migrations, and globalized capitalism, diverse populations increasingly find themselves living together, stuck with one another (Young, 1996, p. 126) and must figure out how to coexist, interact, and thrive together, drawing on their differences as resources rather than obstacles.

FRAMING THE DIALOGUE (JEN)

Here, we take up the idea of being *stuck together*. This conversation stemmed from a quote of Iris Marion Young's (1997, 2002, 2011) about polity—the ways that strangers find themselves interdependently connected with one other. Initially, the notion of being "stuck together" didn't quite sit well with Bob.

Bob's Take

As you'll read in a moment, Jen's use of the term *stuck together* is rooted in the deep soil of personal experience and scholarly theory. However, I was reacting to the term in a much more day-to-day and conversational sense, and those connections were giving me dissonance. The concept of being stuck together conjured up images for me of someone saying to someone else in a resigned way, "Oh well, I guess we're just stuck together," the implied meaning being that they wish it weren't so, but here we are nevertheless. To me, being *stuck together* felt just a tad better than being *stuck with,* but neither term made me sense a welcoming relationship.

It's the *stuck* part that troubling. There's nothing voluntary about it, nor does it suggest movement of any kind. Instead, I see tires stuck in the mud, cars stuck in snow, gum stuck in a toddler's hair, keys stuck in a lock, windows stuck in the frame, fingers stuck in my face. The idea of *stuck together* reminded me of why I and so many educators have issues with the idea of teaching tolerance of other cultures. Teaching tolerance is such a low bar to set. If I tolerate something or someone, I'm barely disguising my dislike for it and merely putting up with it. True, tolerance is better than aggression, but far below acceptance, understanding, and love. I just felt that when people engage across cultures in daily transactions that they should aspire to more than feeling stuck together.

Jen's Take

I see very nearly everything in relation to the ways any of us might need to call on strangers to share our concerns, to pool resources, to make decisions that affect us all. Perhaps my intellectual commitment to public life stems from my own experiences of strangers in the YMCA parking lot or at a local restaurant calling family services when they saw my stepfather beating me and kicking me. At the time, I didn't even know what I was experiencing was abuse. And these strangers' speaking up did little to change anything in my home after the social worker came to ask what seemed to me such strange and paralyzing questions. Later, however, the strangers' willingness to mark what they saw mattered to me; I was their concern. They thought something about what they saw should not be merely a private matter with my family. They saw themselves connected to me, to my family—at least long enough to confront my step-dad and file a complaint, marshaling the few resources they had available to them.

This abbreviated, glossed-over memory illustrates something of Iris Marion Young's concept of *polity.* Based on the Greek notion of *polis* or city, *polity* focuses on the ways we are geographically and economically interdependent—stuck together—with strangers who may be quite different from us. As Bob recognizes, being stuck with others is not always a pleasant affair, and often not of our choosing. It wasn't for me with my stepfather; I don't think the strangers in the parking lot really wanted to be stuck with our family either.

And yet, if a policy informing, say, quality control of water in Flint, Michigan, is not working for some people, those folks need to be able to get others in Flint or beyond Flint to share that concern if anything is going to change. This is also true in relation to some of our most private experiences, like domestic abuse or child abuse or which bodies can use which bathrooms at school or at McDonald's. The likely fact is that others around us—in our towns, in our schools, in our churches and mosques and synagogues, in our economies, in our mayor's office—do not share our experiences or our perspectives, and perhaps don't agree with us or necessarily think they have any reason on their own to pay attention to someone like us. They haven't necessarily *chosen* us; we are strangers—strange and unknown to each other.

But clean water, safe buses, school funding, and more all depend on us being able to construct what Michael Warner (2002) calls *stranger relationality*— productive and generous ways of relating from a stance of wonder and delight—that relies on far more than mere tolerance. With regard to being stuck together, this also means we must construct some reason to share each other's concerns, especially concerns that might not directly impact us but that have a profound impact on the people we're, in one way or another, stuck with. In this way, I see being stuck with one another as deeply connected to the ways we discuss ideological environments and ideological becoming in the remainder of this chapter.

This question of what to do with each other's differences is not an easy one; it is born of struggle, of the difficulties any of us face in carving out a path for ourselves and those we care about while also honoring others' differences that somehow rub against our own. While the struggle for understanding across differences may be inevitable, the struggle itself is neither a deficit nor a thing to dread or to avoid. On the contrary, according to Bakhtin, the social interactions that are most effective in promoting meaning making, and thus, learning, are those that are filled with tension and struggle. "After all," Bakhtin writes, "our thought itself— philosophical, scientific, artistic—is born and shaped in the process of interaction and struggle with others' thought" (1986, p. 92). The wobble that unsettles learners can be a site for growth; it is, at the very least, rife with possibility, and we who educate should come to see and embrace it as such.

You'll notice that we've just equated meaning making with learning. In an era of standardization that increasingly brackets differences and frames learning as a quantifiable product to be delivered and neatly measured, we instead consider what it might mean to embrace the uncertainty and conflict that sometimes accompanies difference and what might be entailed in making struggle a site of learning and growth, of developing ideas and compassion, of inventing, and of becoming. To do this, we put Bakhtinian theories of ideological becoming in conversation with Hermans and Hermans-Konopka's notions of positioning and counter-positioning to consider implications of dialogical self theory for learning in a globalizing society. Why we do this is to ultimately choose—and it is a choice—to look at the cosmos of our classrooms with eyes of wonder. We invite you to remember with us why the work educators do is so lively, why working with young people is such an honor, and why, with stakes so high, we can't consider doing less.

Cultures, Learning, and Ideological Becoming

Bakhtin recognized all language as ideological. He described languages as "specific points of view on the world, forms for conceptualizing the world in words, specific world views" (1981, pp. 291–292). It is worth noting that:

> [t]he Russian "ideologiya" is less politically coloured than the English word "ideology." In other words, it is not necessarily a consciously held political belief system; rather it can refer in a more general sense to the way in which members of a given social group view the world. It is in this broader sense that Bakhtin uses the term. For Bakhtin, any utterance is shot through with "ideologiya," any speaker is automatically an "ideolog."
>
> *(Morris, 1994, p. 249)*

An ideology, for Bakhtin, reflects the hopes, values, desires, and logics of the group. It is a system of ideas that come to mean something to the group about the way the world hangs together (Emerson, 1981, p. 23), whether that group sees the world in strictly political terms or not. And whether or not there are shades of meaning and difference within the group, or we would add, within a person.

Learning literacies, no matter how those literate practices are situated and shared—whether in academic disciplines or home cultures or elsewhere—is as much about cultural ideas and perspectives as it is about words. Language, and thus ideas, become one's own when they are appropriated and adapted for one's own intentions. However, words and ideas do not simply lie dormant or neutral or impersonal, waiting for us to put them to use. They are, rather, "in other people's mouths, in other people's contexts, serving other people's intentions: it is from there that one must take the word, and make it one's own" (Bakhtin, 1981, pp. 293–294). Language, according to Bakhtin, lives an active and engaged life, as it were, forever being simultaneously tugged toward unification while alternately undergoing widespread individualization.

In this sense, language is never static or neutral, but is forever in a process of renewal, a process predicated on response. And language users are ever in a process of renewing language and learning to make ideas and language their own—putting the ideas of others to work in a new way, to fashion a new word, a new world, a new way of seeing for one's own purposes. A person's process of making meaning in relation to the hopes, values, and ideas of others is what Bakhtin called ideological becoming (1981). To foster ideological becoming is to nurture the development of an ideological self with ways of viewing the world and ways of understanding and performing positionings and values that interact and align—or don't—with others.

Putting ideas and words to our own uses requires that we become aware of and respond to the ideas and languages we encounter, and that we position ourselves, our ideas, our ways of using words in relation to others, their ideas, and the ways they use words. Doing this requires a kind of consciousness—a consciousness that can only come into being by becoming aware of the ideas that surround us and shape us. Ideological becoming is, then, perhaps best understood in ideological environments (Bakhtin & Medvedev, 1978, p. 14) where diverse people come together. After all, we are surrounded by "ideological phenonema" (Bakhtin, 1981, p. 14)—words, scientific statements, mascots, statues, religious symbols and beliefs, and so on—that are always changing. Attending to these phenomena in order to see and understand different positions and values in the world and the ways they relate contributes to the development of a person's system of ideas—a system that is always in relation to other people and their systems of ideas. We are arguing, then, to see our material worlds in general and schools in particular as ideological environments that invite dialogic response and foster ideological becoming of a dialogical self.

Ideological Becoming within Ideological Environments

Taking a closer look at our school buildings might help us see ideological environments at work. Consider, for example, a school TESL scholar Rachel Pinnow calls Myers Middle School, built in 1993 in the southeastern US after an influx of Latino families to a previously White, previously pastoral community. Over the next decade or two, the community became a "multicultural, multilingual township" (Pinnow, 2015, p. 12) with Myers reflecting the town's changing demographics with just over half of the school's 900 students self-identifying as White and just under half as Latino/Hispanic.

The signs in the school building—as well as the practices, documents, daily schedule, dress code, and so on—revealed ways of viewing the world and revealed them in dialogue. At the main entrance of the school where students, teachers, and parents alike had to walk past video cameras and glass administrative offices to enter or exit the building, a poster announced in bold stenciled capital letters, "PATRIOTS ARE RISING STARS" against a backdrop of the school's colors of red, white, and blue floating in the shape of the stars and stripes of the US national flag.

The poster, of course—intended primarily for parents, students, and visitors—oriented students as people on their way to future success and as "patriots," the school's official mascot. Of course, red, white, and blue on the signs connects students to the US flag, "invoke[ing] nationalistic notions of membership throughout the school" (Pinnow, 2015, p. 13). This poster pointed to a system of ideas about the work of school and about the young people who come through the door. It suggested the school's commitment to student achievement (Pinnow, 2015, p. 12) as well as a socializing commitment to instilling national loyalty. The 'Patriot' mascot was originally depicted as a revolutionary war figure who held a rifle in his hands. The illustration—either subtly or overtly, depending on your view— suggested that "patriots," as the students were referred to in signs throughout the school, are, or should be, aggressive, military fighters prepared to use weapons in the name of loyalty, pride, or nationalism.

Signs like the one at the front entrance and mascot images in lunchrooms or gymnasiums are common in schools across the country. Sometimes they just seem to blend into the background and appear normal and neutral. And yet, they are ideological, and often are interpreted differently by different people. Angela Dean (2016), a teacher in northeast Georgia, tells of walking the halls during the teacher preparation days before school begins for the year and noticing a trend in posters that many of her colleagues had adopted. The posters, she hoped, were meant to be inspirational—a wet cat clinging to a clothesline with "Hang in there, baby" as the caption or a majestic eagle soaring toward the mountaintop—but Angela began to wonder about what other messages were being communicated.

In particular, one kind of poster, which Angela often saw prominently placed next to pencil sharpeners or by entryways, shouted in bold letters, "The attitude STOPS here!" She wondered how such posters—which seemed to cast any student as having a bad attitude—created spaces in which dialogue was devalued. If the posters were the only such message sent by the school, then perhaps their power would easily be nullified by other more dialogical actions and processes. However, Angela also noted how an administrator constantly harangued students over the speaker system to empty the halls as soon as school ended or how cafeteria workers belittled students who wore their pants too low on their hips.

In all these instances, students had very little leverage with which to engage in dialogue; the only expected response was compliance. When confronted with a range of messages in an ideological environment that had few if any expectations for dialogue, Angela worried that students would, under this negative tension, develop the bad attitudes the posters were meant to prevent. Moreover, how does the teacher who is trying to teach in dialogical ways overcome the resistance built up by these more monological encounters that have taken place before students even enter her class?

Perhaps part of a positive response to Angela's concern lies in the fluidity of language and culture, as we have been discussing. Sometimes a change in context can bring the ideologies of the artifacts that surround us into sharp relief. A poster in the hall or a painting of a mascot in the school gym, seemingly innocuous one day, can suddenly take on new meanings the next. After the Columbine High School shootings in 1999, the teachers and parents affiliated with Myers School saw the rifle carried by the Patriot mascot in a new light. Soon afterward, the rifle was painted over with a US flag.

Although neither the mascot nor his rifle had ever been neutral, the massacre at Columbine suddenly made the lack of neutrality more evident to more people;

it was an image that carried values and meanings, values and meanings that perhaps might be harmful. In changing the appearance of the mascot, the school marked the potential role of ideological phenomena in ideological becoming as well as its own culpability in fostering particular values. While the aggressive posture and facial expression of the Patriot were not changed, clearly, adults connected to Myers School came to see the Patriot carrying a rifle as a value they no longer wanted to promote. Indeed, they may not have previously thought of the rifle as ideological at all.

Of course, we need to note, that the stakeholders at Myers School traded one ideologically saturated image for another. In their defense, they couldn't help but do so, given that all language, image, and action are ideologically saturated. But, we think it important to point out they had choices as to how they wanted the Patriot depicted and what message they wanted the image to convey. We wonder what alternatives they might have considered, if they considered alternatives at all, to the American flag. What if the rifle were exchanged for a Bible? What ideological thinking would be behind such a move? Consider this choice: instead of a flag, the Patriot could be holding a fife or beating a drum. What if his arms encircled his family? Or a Latino and Native American? What ideological message would be sent if the Patriot mascot were a woman? What if the Patriot were depicted as an African American? Could we imagine the Patriot holding nothing, instead standing open-handed, maybe reaching out?

In considering the range of options available even in this one scenario, it becomes clear that despite a less politically charged concept of "ideologiya," ideological becoming does not exclude hierarchies, value judgments, and power dynamics from ideological development. Indeed, politics are an integral part of using language and of learning together. Interestingly, as immigrant populations grew in the town and school, Myers continued to promote the Patriot as a mascot, even denoting the school as "Patriot country"—a term that, coupled with the White, male revolutionary war figure, "contribute[d] to the establishment of 'us' and 'them' political classifications (i.e., those who are patriots and those who are not) and nationalism based on land and borders (i.e., 'country')" (Pinnow, p. 16). Certainly, these signs implied that loyalty to the US was more desirable than loyalty to another place or another heritage or another culture—a significant political statement and value judgment to make in a school and a town with a growing immigrant population.

These implications, however, are even more significant and complicated in light of a range of immigrants' generational responses to the idea of assimilation or integration or incorporation, or any word to describe the process of belonging. A first-generation immigrant will usually struggle with more cultural differences than his American-born child. Some first-generation immigrants, especially those who have sought refuge in the US from harsh, and they hope temporary, circumstances back home harbor the "myth of return" (La Vecchia-Mikkola, 2011). Although there are significant differences across civic, cultural, economic, and emotional assimilation among immigrant populations (Hanes, 2013), second-generation immigrants are more likely to see themselves as "typical Americans" (Pew Study Social Trends, 2013) even though some nonimmigrant Americans may not hold that view. Later immigrant generations often experience what has been termed "the immigrant paradox": educational success sometimes declines even though English fluency rises; social mobility tends to flatten out; and health of immigrant children often declines (North, 2009). Some later-generation immigrants embrace their historic, cultural, and linguistic heritage, reconnecting with family members, stories, languages, and cultural practices that may have been lost or set aside by second-generation immigrants. If this weren't complex enough, assimilation itself is conflicted, multidimensional, and multidirectional (Skerry, 2000).

The dialogue stirred by a sign in a school hallway is often far from simple or straightforward. Immigrant and nonimmigrant youth, as well as their teachers, are in dialogue with a range of voices, histories, alliances, and homelands. And yet many of the ideological phenomena young people encounter in school promote one voice or history or homeland, one place of belonging, one way of belonging. This, of course, is no accident.

Remember Said's point that cultural artifacts and aesthetics taught in schools and displayed in institutions reflect what a culture upholds as beautiful and right and form a basis by which all other stories and art forms—and their cultures—are evaluated. These ideological phenomena also do the work of creating norms, structuring relationships, and creating a particular sense of order. They help to shape "kinds of people" (Hacking, 2007).

Consider another example from a classroom across the country in Arizona, where ethnic studies were banned in schools and anti-immigration legislation received national attention. On the classroom wall, a district-sponsored poster reads, "The only violence in schools should be the kind you read about in history classes. Be smart. Don't become history." On the poster, a picture of a history textbook is opened to a page titled "Civil War" (Paris, 2012, p. 6). The poster suggests to the students at the primarily Latina/o school: "Be smart. Don't become history. Leave history in books. History is in the past. Violence is in the past. The Civil War, that violent battle for, among other things, human rights, is in the past. Leave it there. Such struggles are not a part of school" (Paris, 2012, p. 6).

And yet, Arizona lawmakers *had* made the struggle part of school, raiding homes of Latina/o students who might be "suspicious" and banning Mexican American studies courses in schools. As writer–activist Tony Diaz noted, "It's clear to me that our intellectual advancement is a threat to some people, because they tried to make it illegal." When the case was taken before the 9th Circuit Court of Appeals, it became obvious that the ban was also meant to include Asian and African American Studies in addition to Mexican American Studies. When the judges asked the Arizona counsel, "Suppose you had a class in Chinese language, one that helps Chinese students, would that be illegal in Arizona?" the lawyer for the state of Arizona answered, "Yes" (Diaz, 2015).

Young people are, whether they realize it or not, engaged in a dynamic process of ideological becoming. They encounter a range of competing, often conflicting, overlapping ideological phenomena that can at times seem neutral but that never operate simply—or neutrally—"as information, directions, rules, models and so forth—but striv[e] to determine the very basis of our ideological interrelations with the world, the very basis of [their] behavior" (Bakhtin, 1981, p. 342). These phenomena are deeply connected to cultures, simultaneously emerging from cultural practices and reproducing cultural practices and ideologies. Young people, who come to school with ways of being, thinking, believing, talking, writing, and so on that mark them as members of certain cultures, as certain "kinds of people" (Hacking, 2007), are continually faced with possibilities and pressures to identify with certain cultural ways—including school ways—or to "loop back" and rewrite or move away from particular cultural practices and ideologies.

In April of 2010, the Arizona Legislature passed State Bill 1070 that made it a state crime to be undocumented and required police to check papers of those they viewed with "reasonable suspicion" of being undocumented. On the day Governor Jan Brewer was slated to sign the bill into law, students across metro Phoenix left their schools to march on the capitol in protest. The night before, a Latina sent out a text message (rendered faithfully here): "WALK OUT! ALL SCHOOLS Thursday april 22, Fuck Bill SB1070! Stop the racial profiling, Stop this injustice! We walk at 11am and were marching." Students rallied, forwarded the message, and prepared to walk out the next day. A concerned mother gave her son Pedro a megaphone and told him, "Don't get deported." Pedro responded, "We're doing this for you" (Paris, 2012 p. 7). The day of the protest, students carried signs—"Veto SB1070!" "Arizona Stop SB1070"—and chanted "El pueblo, unido, jamas sera vencido!" ("The people united will never be defeated").

Later in an interview, Pedro would connect his participation in the march to a longer history of struggling for civil and human rights:

> Remember the time that Martin Luther King and them were marching … They got sprayed with water and everything, they still didn't care. They still fought for their rights … I think that if they're trying to racial profile us and nobody does nothing about it, someone has to step up. And the people that stepped up for us, it was us, the students. We're the ones that stepped up because we were the first ones that didn't move, not the adults or nothing. We were the ones that took our choice and we started marching downtown to make a difference.
>
> (Paris, 2012, p. 8)

For Pedro, protesting SB1070 meant engaging in dialogue on many fronts: the self, school personnel, fellow students, parents, heritage, lawmakers, historical precedence, and no doubt more. He was immersed in an eddy of dialogue where all involved were voicing perspectives that were ideologically saturated. Yet he began to populate those perspectives with his own intentions.

For Bakhtin, ideological becoming—generative processes by which we develop our own ways of viewing the world—occurs within these "contact zones" (Bakhtin, 1986, p. 14). As Bakhtin uses the phrase, "contact zones" are where one culture's system of ideas and values afford or constrain certain ways of being that are valued and performed quite differently in another culture's system of ideas. Contact zones—whether they occur in classrooms, at the neighborhood park, in the workplace, on the metro—are not only physical arrangements of materials, resources, signs, and symbols but also key socializing spaces. In contact zones we, and the young people we teach, learn how others are oriented toward us and toward our cultures and ideas, and we learn to navigate and negotiate various discourses, positions, and degrees of authority.

In contact zones where diverse voices interact, Bakhtin (1981) argued that we struggle to assimilate two distinct categories of discourse: (a) authoritative discourse and (b) internally persuasive discourse. Authoritative discourse is "so to speak, the word of the fathers. Its authority was already acknowledged in the past. It is a prior discourse. It is therefore not a question of choosing it among other possible discourses that are its equal" (Bakhtin, 1981). Speakers of such discourse intend it only to be complied with or rejected. There is no intent, on their part, for dialogue, for other perspectives, for contingencies, for alternate views. It is or it isn't.

Authoritative discourse often emanates from recognized power centers and invokes a recognized official discourse—like the discourse of science or of religious dogma or of policy—that borrows its power and legitimacy from history, tradition, acknowledged beliefs, or voices of authority. An authoritative discourse doesn't necessarily need to flex its authority in order to maintain its perceived authority. Its reliance on cultural values and histories is generally enough to sustain the perceived legitimacy of an authoritative discourse for cultural insiders. Although it can seem normal or neutral to those who acknowledge the official line, the authoritative word insists on assimilation, conformity, obedience, "that we acknowledge it, that we make it our own" regardless of "any power it might have to persuade us internally" (Bakhtin, 1981, p. 342).

When the principal told Jared and Pascale they could not dress in drag for homecoming, the declaration, at least from the principal's stance and perception, was an authoritative word that set the tone, established the norms, laid the ground rules. The principal carried an expectation—based on the nominative authority ascribed to the office more by historical and cultural positioning than any direct series of formative transactions on his part—that the principal's voice and words were pronouncements to be followed rather than suggestions to be considered.

In part because an authoritative word presents itself as acknowledged common sense or matter-of-fact policy, we don't typically struggle against authoritative discourses unless we've experienced, and found compelling, an alternative discourse that does not align with the authoritative discourse. Or until, in a particular context at a particular moment, we find ourselves as individuals not quite grooving with some aspect of an official doctrine that we had until that moment experienced as authoritative, matter-of-fact, and unquestioned.

Think about the response to the Patriot mascot after the Columbine massacre. Surely, some of the community members who insisted on changing the image of the Patriot mascot must have experienced moments of wrestling with a deep-seated authoritative discourse of national patriotism that, until the Columbine massacre, had seemed both matter-of-fact and a legitimate expression of loyalty and heritage. Authoritative discourses sometimes emerge in the speech of authorities, like Jared and Pascale's principal, or in traditions, like homecoming celebrations; more often, authoritative discourses circulate in far more ambient ways, underpinning practices that in turn reproduce those discourses. For this reason, authoritative discourses can sometimes be difficult to pinpoint or recognize—especially if a person also finds them internally persuasive—until something jarring disrupts, makes visible, and calls into question the value-laden ideology that previously was experienced as innocuous or even common sense.

Besides struggling with the official authoritative discourses circulating, we also come into contact with and struggle with the everyday discourses of individuals we encounter in our daily lives—discourses adopted and adapted from multiple cultures we encounter and reassemble to be our own. These everyday discourses are what Bakhtin called internally persuasive discourses—what each person thinks for himself or herself, what ultimately is persuasive to the individual, even if only momentarily persuasive. Unlike authoritative discourse, internally persuasive discourse is "denied all privilege, backed by no authority at all, and is frequently not even acknowledged in society" (1981, p. 342). It has no external center of power. Instead, "it is affirmed through assimilation, tightly interwoven with one's own words" (Bakhtin, 1981, p. 345). When voters tune into several televised debates in order to capture the range of discussion, when students doing a project for school engage a number of diverse and divergent websites focused on their topic, when couples weigh the options of having children, when a teacher encourages text-based, but alternate views on a novel—all are engaging in internally persuasive discourse.

By dialoguing across a range of ideological environments, we continually encounter discourses that further unify or further destabilize our worldviews. As learners, we need to be pulled in both directions. However, as we pointed out through the examples in this section, too often schools are skewing past unification toward reification of expectation and meaning. In other words, dialogue is too often quashed when the discourse of school is heavy-handed or unquestioned; when policy is rendered in authoritative discourse, pronouncements can only be obeyed or rejected.

To see discourse—authoritative and internally persuasive—as ideological is also to recognize the need for questioning, evaluating, deliberating, reassembling, and repurposing discourses. As educators, rather than relying on authoritative discourse that either pretends to neutrality or flexes power, we might consider ways of opening up dialogue, even in transactions that might otherwise result in a stand-off—not for the purposes of persuasion but to put the different ideologies we carry with us and see around us into conversation in order to reassemble new possibilities for being and becoming.

When people speak or write, even in the matter-of-fact language of procedure, they reveal their developing ideologies and positionings, and their points of reference. In the texts they read—dress codes, rubrics, classrooms posters—as well as the ones they create, young people interpret for themselves and others their own locations in cultural contexts, how others would position them and how they would position themselves. They leave traces of intertwined authoritative utterances and discourses—picking up, abandoning, appropriating, connecting, transforming the discourses of others in ways that reflect their awareness of their ever-changing social positions, ideologies, and available actions in various contexts (Maguire & Graves, 2001). Drawing attention to and valuing the multiplicity of cultures and voices that young people embody opens up possibilities for expansive ways of thinking and being and invites youth to think carefully and critically about being in productive dialogue with themselves and others, marking these dialogues as important sites of learning.

Imagine, for instance, if administrators had asked Jared and Pascale why they wanted to dress in drag and what mattered so much about being able to do that for homecoming. Or if they'd created a broader inquiry among administrators, student council, and the youth, who might all have very different goals for homecoming. What if they'd talked about contradictory practices—that male alumni can return for an assembly and wear dresses, wigs, and make-up in a staged pageant but a male student elected to homecoming court can't wear a dress to accept the crown? Or if they'd taken a look together at the range of socializing practices in the high school surrounding homecoming, Valentine's Day, prom, and other socially constructed school events and how queer students, Mormon students, Native American students, cisgender and transgender students, and so on, might all experience these differently? Rather than making a site of conflict a site of coercion, these kinds of shifts have the potential to transform a site of conflict and an experience of wobble into a site of inquiry and knowledge-building.

Relationships with the Self in Educational Contexts

One of the main conceptions that we think dialogical self theory (DST) brings to education is an awareness of the self as a dialogical being, as an entity that is simultaneously united and multiple. We are also self-aware enough to suspect that such a statement causes some readers stress, that they become vexed by the idea that a person can construct an identity that evokes both unity and multiplicity. Our challenge then is to help all of us become more comfortable with a self that, as Hermans and Hermans-Konopka (2010) discussed, can "make the notion of unity and continuity fit" with the acknowledgment of "difference, multiplicity, contradiction, and

Dialogical Self theory (DST)

discontinuity" (p. 9) all residing within that unity and continuity. By honoring this complex construction of self, we open ourselves as teachers and, subsequently, our students to learning situations that are nuanced, contextual, social, and fluid.

One way to imagine what occurs within a dialogical self is to consider the idea that, as folks are able to develop relationships with other folk, so too they can develop relationships with themselves. After all, "relationships that emerge *between* people can also emerge *within* the self" (Hermans and Hermans-Konopka, 2010 p. 120, emphasis in original). In some ways, these relationships we build with ourselves are similar to relationships we build with others. They are tentative yet substantive, of the moment yet historical, individual yet social, solidifying yet responsive. Familiar indications of such relationships pepper our language: she's comfortable in her own skin; I can live with myself; I'm of two minds about that issue; my head says go, but my heart says stay. Phrases such as these all point to a sense of well-being, acceptance, tolerance, division, disappointment, or a list of other modifiers that would indicate how we view either our whole or some aspect of our self. Of that range of dialogical relationships within the self, four seem quite prevalent and useful for our discussion: self-conflict, self-criticism, self-agreement, and self-consultancy (Hermans & Hermans-Konopka, 2010).

Self-conflict

Most of us experience some degree of self-conflict in our daily lives, whether we're weighing what to order off the menu, deciding what story to include in the next unit we teach, determining whether or not to take a job, or wrestling with the possibility of getting a divorce. Sometimes the conflict is seemingly minor and temporary as with the menu, but sometimes we experience an extended and perhaps painful "war of voices" as with a job or a divorce. Sometimes the consequences are relatively minor. There is likely no serious difference in our menu preferences. Sometimes the choices we feel conflicted about create turmoil precisely because the consequences are quite serious and the differences in the options we voice to ourselves quite pronounced.

Many people tend to bring strong negative connotations to the word *conflict*, connecting it to war, confrontation, and upheaval. Regarding their lives, we suspect many might wish it would go away. Although we are not advocating a life lived in conflict, we are also not advocating a life devoid of conflict. Out of conflict, frequently comes creativity and new perspectives. When Bakhtin (1984) wrote about the medieval carnival—a time when, through anonymous play in the streets, the hierarchies of the world could be momentarily suspended—he explained how such an event involved "feasts of becoming ... hostile to all that was immortalized and complete." The parodic humor of the feasts was intended to be in conflict with and to call into question the reigning social order. On a more contemporary stage, the satiric work of such people as Jon Stewart, Stephen Colbert, Tig Notaro, and John Oliver starts at the identification of an ideological or personal conflict and then lifts that conflict up for examination in ways that simultaneously entertain, unnerve, and inform. In similar ways, conflict within the self calls attention—creates a wobble moment, if you will—and provokes us to not only pay attention, but frequently to act. To admit to the self-conflict is to admit to opportunity to move in new directions.

Adolescents in contemporary classrooms frequently undergo much self-conflict. In our example of Pascale and Jared, it's easy to imagine them being conflicted over wanting to respect authority, even one they find unreasonable, and wanting to take a parodic stance on homecoming while simultaneously celebrating their identities in process. Frequently other youth find themselves caught between honoring the wish of their parents that they go to law school and their own wish to apprentice to a timber frame carpenter or try organic farming. It is within classrooms—through dialogical inquiry into the essential questions of life—that young learners may gain substantive and nuanced insight into the conflicts that unsettle them.

Teachers can also introduce mild forms of conflict within classrooms by nudging students with classic opened-ended questions: Why do you believe that assertion you just made? Where is your evidence for that thought? Why do you think the protagonist is a coward? What leads you to that conclusion? How do you think someone else hearing that statement might react? There's nothing magical here. But such questions cause momentary wobble because they unsettle the responder. The expectation is "Tell us more; you've only touched on the surface." As a facilitator of such dialogue, you leaven the level of conflict through your tone. Such questions should not be issued as rebukes, but rather as invitations to enter the dialogue in more substantive ways. And you always look for ways to bring others in the class into the dialogue, perhaps asking others to chime in or, perhaps better because it engages all in the room, asking everyone to take a few minutes to write on a question that has manifested through the discussion.

Self-criticism

If you've ever thought to yourself, "I can't believe I just did that!" or told yourself that you just said something "stupid," you were engaging in self-criticism. These are fairly typical expressions of self-evaluation and self-correction. Bob's step-daughter Erin used to always find amusement in what became known as "Robert moments," episodes when having done something absentmindedly or in error such as spilling soda or getting soaked by an ill-aimed hose, Bob would chastise himself by shouting, "Robert." Such mild reproaches are common and generally people express their self-critique when, according to either self- or other imposed standards, they feel they've fallen short.

Sometimes self-criticism is more temporary, like when you wish you hadn't just put your foot in your mouth, and at other times is more extended, such as at a critical life transition or during self-reflection that often accompanies old age.

Meta-cognition (handwritten note)

In these moments, self-awareness also involves self-evaluation. Certainly, self-evaluation that leads to self-condemnation can cause an immense amount of pain, but this division of self need not be abusive and, in fact, can be both healing and productive. In self-criticism, there is an opportunity to reflexively consider who we've been and what we've done in the past, to become more aware of the standards we are measuring ourselves against, to learn from past decisions and circumstances, and to consider the values and wisdom we hope to carry forward.

Given the current regime of standardization in so many public schools, it's hard for us to imagine students or teachers having much time and space to engage in thoughtful self-reflection and critique. Pacing schedules and seemingly incessant testing barely give students and teachers opportunities to breathe let alone reflect and critique, nor do they allow them time and opportunity to self-select what standards they'll be held to. Yet, as Donald Schön (1984) indicated, reflection on practice is what experienced and expert professionals do. The entire practitioner researcher movement is predicated on the idea that teachers improve their practice when they, as Cochran-Smith and Lytle (2009) have indicated, consider systematically and intentionally what is happening in their classrooms. Looking toward the needs of students, learning to write, to read, and to research is critically aided by metacognition, an ability to think about and reflect on what you're thinking.

Ian Altman (2016), a teacher in a Georgia high school, goes so far as to model self-critique in a way that also demonstrates lateral thinking (de Bono, 2015), or the ability to think flexibly or in multiple ways about problems or issues. Altman, who is a teacher activist for un(der)documented students, will take an Op Ed piece that he has written for a local paper—one in which he supports the rights of un(der) documented students to higher education—and a piece written on the same subject by a conservative commenter, and assign students to critique the arguments of one or the other. Additionally, Altman takes great fun in picking apart his own arguments. The upshot is that students get an opportunity to see that all writing, even that which you write yourself, is open to multiple interpretations.

To use a colloquialism, beating up on yourself is never useful; it's self-demeaning and indicative of self-loathing. But to never be self-critical—to not reflect and reconsider your thoughts and actions—is to never place yourself into a position for progressive change. To never pay heed to that which may be wobbling in our learning is to diminish our ongoing construction of a self in mindful pursuit of meaning. Classrooms, with their ever-changing contexts in terms of depth of understanding and the deluge of easily accessible and often contradictory sites of information, cry out for moments of stillness devoted to considering who we have been, who we are, and who we are becoming.

Self-agreement

As a quick reminder, the self is composed of many I-positions, what Hermans and Hermans-Konopka (2010) have characterized as a "society of mind" (p. 62), one that is simultaneously tugged by localizing and globalizing forces. Forces of local-ization serve to center the mind, bringing a greater sense of unity to the many I-positions. Such unification is healthy up to a point, but can lead to closing the self off from diversity and innovation. Forces of globalization tend to decenter and diversify the many I-positions, providing these various facets of the self with richer and fuller input into decision-making. However, if overdone, such decen-tering leads to a sense of instability and fragmentation. You can hear the echoes of Bakhtin's (1981) work on language at play here. Similarly to language, the self functions best when some equilibrium between unification and individualization can be achieved.

The dialogical concept of self-agreement acts somewhat like a negotiator among our various I-positions, seeking some measure of consensus. In moments of self-agreement, we make negotiations in which one part of our selves is regu-lating and attempting to coax, persuade, bargain with, make promises to, or reward another part of ourselves. Rather than a monological stance in which one part of the self forces another part of the self to do something it doesn't want to do, self-agreement involves a kind of internal deliberation where I-positions negotiate an option that is workable for the different parts of the self, even if the different parts are in agreement for different reasons. You've engaged in this kind of negotiation if you've said something like, "Well, I was hesitant at first, but I talked myself into it" or "I made a deal with myself. If I ran on the treadmill for 30 minutes, I could have dessert."

Within education, self-agreements can be a means for dealing with the work of learning, not necessarily the busy work of mindless worksheets and drills, but the thoughtful and complex projects that, although are work, hold much intel-lectual and emotional reward if done well. For instance, the teacher who, faced with a mountain of essays waiting for feedback, remembers that invariably reading these essays helps her better understand the perspectives of her students and brings her closer to them. Thus motivated, she gets to work. Or the young writer who, in deciding between a night of online gaming and completing an assigned per-sonal narrative, figures out a way to use the former as a reward for getting started on the latter. In these moments of self-negotiation, we construct frameworks for future cycles of learning.

Self-consultancy

At times when we must make difficult decisions or make sense of a complex and perplexing problem or choose a course of action that might carry serious implications for ourselves or others, we sometimes consult with ourselves to try to walk ourselves through possibilities. Self-consultancy sometimes involves self-interrogation, in which one part of the self poses a question and accesses a different part of the self, sometimes a part more quiet and less conscious. In self-consultancy, a person often needs extended time and solitude to mull things over and to give less immediately accessible parts of the self a chance to weigh in and emerge with a response.

Hermans and Hermans-Konopka (2010) described self-consultancy as occurring at the "interface of the conscious and unconscious levels of the mind" (p. 126), meaning that we're not always aware of what I-positions we're accessing in the consultation. Most of us who teach have had the experience of going to sleep vexed by an issue or concerned about a struggling student only to wake up with a clear-headed plan of action or a sense of how to proceed. As we consult with ourselves, we seek out the range of experience that crosses our many I-positions. For example, I-the-acoustic-guitar-player might have insight into the issues of I-the-science-teacher, if I let the guitar player into the conversation. Mary Catherine Bateson (2010) tells of an accomplished friend, Ruth, who, nevertheless, worried about her ability to be successful at a prestigious graduate school. In a classic example of self-consultancy, Ruth explained, "I had to convince myself that [my ability to achieve] was not an issue, and did" (p. 48).

As we work with students, then, it would be wise to create opportunities for them to grapple with complexity and to support their efforts to self-consult their way toward creative responses, knowing that pursuing these intentions will take time and support. Doing so—allowing time to play a role in the ongoing work of a classroom—may feel risky to many teachers. Time, they feel, is a finite commodity, one they never have enough of. The clock on pacing schedules and standardized testing starts ticking on the first day of school and only clicks louder as the year goes on. Such subtle and not so subtle pressure to get all the content covered in X amount of minutes, days, or weeks often pushes even the best teachers into a race to keep pace and cover material rather than teach it in depth and well.

Accordingly, we ask teachers to self-consult, to acknowledge the pull toward center that expects conformity and then to imagine individual and collective resistance to the centering force, to instead develop ways to slow down rather than speed up the curriculum. The answer may lie in sacrificing some concepts for the sake of others you determine to be more important. It may involve thinking more creatively about how to combine a number of mandated and diverse standards under one or a series of projects that, by being connected, create more opportunities for prolonged engagement. The idea is to see the self with its many I-positions as one of the first resources that teachers and students consult when faced with conundrums of teaching and learning.

Thinking across Relationships with the Self

At times, any one of these relationships we construct with our self may be more dominant than others. For instance, while contending with a dying parent who has left vague instructions regarding life support situations, we might find ourselves in conflict between trying to relieve the suffering of a loved one, wanting to preserve our time with them, and needing to attend to other aspects of our lives. Losing a parent may call up issues of what it means for I-the-child to continue constructing a life in which a mother or father or both may no longer be physically present. And sometimes we close ourselves off from or are in denial about a relationship. We elect not to self-critique, for instance, when we fear what such self-critique might unearth.

Like we do with their external counterparts, we frequently shuffle through a range of relationships with our many I-positions across a given time period. The bottom line is that such relationships are common and reveal themselves in a variety of ways. These relationships within the self reveal some ways the self tries to navigate its own multiplicity. They also show that at times parts of the self are immediately accessible, that other parts require more time and quiet and concentrated effort to access, and that some parts may say or do or think something that the self as a unifying whole is unsure about. This dialogue is deeply connected to the cultures we find ourselves part of, the "kinds of people" (Hacking, 2007) those cultures value, and the ways we come to know those values through ideological phenomena that carry the authoritative discourses and internally persuasive discourses of others.

In real time as a clash of cultures plays out in the classroom or in the principal's office or in the cafeteria or on the basketball court, a person is intent on the action at hand and has little opportunity to reflect on or even to be aware of the complex dialogue that is unfolding. Previous discourses may condition quick and familiar responses. In classrooms, teachers often have routines precisely for this purpose: to avoid losing precious class time, teachers limit decision-making so that certain ways of coming into the classroom or transitioning into and out of groups become habit because a prior decision has been made—usually by the teacher—about the best way to do this. These quick responses, whether they happen in routinized situations or high-speed athletic contests or chaotic cafeteria clashes, do not usually allow for much, if any reflection or dialogue.

However, if we engage young people in the work of ideological becoming, we need to provide opportunities for youth to make sense of the world unfolding around them, opportunities for them to freeze-frame (Clifton & Sigoloff, 2013) and reflect on the many dialogues they are part of whether they realize it or not. Consider Hermans and Hermans-Konopka's (2010) example of a tennis player: As long as she is performing in the match, her full attention is focused on the action. In the action, she is in the I-position of player caught up in her moment-to-moment performance. To not, as is often said, have her head in the game, is to further jeopardize her chances of winning. To be troubled about having locked her keys in the car just before the match or to fantasize about the evening to come with a new love interest—to admit I-the-worrier or I-the-romantic onto the court—is to create a bifurcation of focus. She is no longer solely of the moment and of this place, but is intellectually and emotionally spread across other moments and places.

opps for freeze-frame

After the game, she has a chance to remember specific moments and to think about her performance and about herself as a tennis player. She can also engage in a deeper reflection if she puts her position as a tennis player alongside and in conversation with other positions. She might consider connections between or tensions among her position as tennis player and her position as daughter, scholar, ROTC leader, American Sign Language translator, and so on. She might consider her positive relationship as daughter of caring parents as having provided her with a confident attitude necessary for match play or her disciplined ROTC leader position as the source of mental and physical stamina. Conversely, her daughter I-position may never feel it does enough to satisfy demanding parents or the ROTC I-position may wonder about a perceived lack of teamwork. This kind of reflection in which she takes a broader position to consider a range of other positions fosters meta-cognition that opens up a dialogical space among value-laden I-positions and cultures.

CONNECTING TO PRACTICE

The situations young people encounter each day are to some degree familiar and to some degree entirely new, often requiring quick thinking and action in the moment that may at times also seem confusing or feel conflicted. Those encounters that are most important and most perplexing—those in which young people find themselves asking, "What just happened?"—are especially important to revisit for individual reflection and, at times, also for shared inquiry and dialogue. For this kind of meaning making that constructs ideological becoming as a conscious focus of dialogical selves, we offer some approaches for fostering literate practices to scaffold individual and shared inquiry.

Important situations in which we experience uncertainty, conflict, and difference often highlight competing logics, experiences, and cultures informing the ways individuals see themselves, others, and what's going on. Think about the different ways people might experience a gathering at a school flagpole for a Day of Remembrance intended to honor and grieve the lives of queer youth who have been killed or who have committed suicide as a result of bullying. Some students and teachers may be deeply concerned; others may see a gathering of queer youth and their allies not as an expression of solidarity and concern but as a show of "gay pride"; still others may be offended that queer youth would dare to be so visible and vocal at school; still others might not think the gathering matters at all if they don't think gay students are bullied at their school (Clifton & Sigoloff, 2013). At the flagpole or in the hallways afterward, the ways young people talk about this situation might be deeply personal and disturbing for some even as other students make jokes, call their peers "fags," or brush it off.

Other felt difficulties in which multiple perspectives might brush up against each other in similar ways could include those related to school suspension policies, ethnic studies bans, English Only policies, school violence, gendered bathroom policies, the stress of "doing school" (Pope, 2003), standardized testing, and demographic changes. Situations that are differently salient for different students are valuable moments to *freeze-frame* (Clifton & Sigoloff, 2013) and open up for inquiry and dialogue.

Freeze-Framing

Freeze-framing leverages multi-literacies to hit the pause button on a situation that would otherwise pass by in a blur and to richly dramatize the multivoiced complexity of what played out. Freeze-framing allows individuals to get outside a situation and to see it, once written, as an object of study, to take their time and ask again, out of interest and a deep need to understand, What just happened?

However, a simple retelling is not enough to scaffold personal or shared inquiry of selves-in-dialogue. And yet there is something powerful in leveraging narrative to dramatize *critical incidents* (Clifton & Sigoloff, 2013) and inquire into selves-in-dialogue in ways that include multiple stakeholders, offer rich contextual background and social conditions, and elaborate on stakeholders' reasoning. The elaboration of multiple perspectives and the articulation of different lines of reasoning that are often hidden open up those perspectives and logics as objects of inquiry and dialogue.

Cultivating Selves-in-Dialogue

Freeze-framing complex situations and dramatizing critical incidents can foster dialogical reflection within and among multiple stakeholders. Individual students might read the text of a *critical incident* they've written or watch the juxtaposed performances of multiple monologues they've created Anna Deveare Smith-style and then reflect on their selves-in-dialogue:

- Which of my I-positions are most salient in this situation? How does that change as the incident unfolds?
- What experiences or ways of thinking do each of these I-positions raise to the surface for me? As a _____ (student, daughter, teammate, friend, photographer, activist, citizen, scholar...) I am most concerned about ... I find myself thinking about ... I wonder ... I hope ...

- Which of my I-positions seem to be in dialogue with one another? In what way? In which moments, and how, do I experience *self-conflict, self-critique, self-agreement, self-consultancy*?
- What seems to be most resolved to me? Where is there tension or something unresolved among my I-positions?

Valuing Others' Dialogical Selves

Finally, students might consider one other stakeholder in the freeze-framed situation:

- Which I-positions seem most salient to that person in this situation? How does that change as the situation unfolds?
- What does that person see as the "problem" here?
- What would that person most want me to care about as a _____ *(student, daughter, teammate, friend, photographer, activist, citizen, scholar…)?* Would that person ask me to foreground a different I-position than the ones I have so far?

Metacognition among I-positions allows a person to put those positions at arm's length, at least temporarily, to see the relationships among different positions. This kind of reflection is often evaluative, raising questions about what is important to each position and what that has meant for the ways a person has attended to those positions. Perhaps some positions have been quieted or neglected, not only by the self, but by others or by institutions. Reflecting across I-positions also allows a person to see connections between positions as part of a personal history, or as part of a collective cultural history. A person might also become increasingly aware that some positions have become more or less accessible over time, or that one or more positions is important to develop for a future sense of self. This also allows for a broader basis for decision-making, for determining options and values available.

Now, and Then

Remember Cassie, the new teacher whose story we related at the start of this chapter? She was evidencing several simultaneous relationships with her self as her students reacted to the cafeteria situation and district office observers waited for her to get the class started. Certainly, *self-conflict* was occurring as she tried to ferret out whether I-the-authoritarian-teacher or I-the-empathetic-teacher or I-the-district-employee or I-the-curious-observer should rise to the surface. Perhaps not then and there, but certainly afterwards—both immediately and months later in a summer institute run by a local site of the National Writing

Project—Cassie engaged in *self-critique*. In doing so she called up a range of actions she could have taken and put them in dialogue with the actions she did take in an attempt to develop a more nuanced sense of her practice. We suspect that she arrived at some level of *self-agreement* among her conflicted selves by negotiating a pact that allowed her to let the hubbub continue if doing so would allow her time to construct a way for the energy in the room to transition into her lesson. *Self-consultancy*, in this case, might be a bit more difficult to view in overt terms, but we're convinced that Cassie tapped some problem-solving self on the shoulder in her attempt to move class ahead without dousing the energy in the room.

As you reflect on Cassie and the other examples and ideas we've discussed in this chapter, perhaps the main point you are deriving is that education in schools is complex, even hopelessly complex. We worry about that tacked on adverb *hopelessly*. Certainly, in a book aimed toward future and current teachers, our intent is not to fling you into the abyss. We in no way want you to see teaching as a daunting exercise in futility. It would serve you and us no purpose to present the future context of education as being one without hope.

That caution noted, we in no way want to sell you a bill of goods or pull a bait and switch. Teaching is a complex activity and, as we noted earlier, complexity, does not lend itself to solutions. Rarely, if ever, do we alter a complex situation with finality, in a wipe-the-dust-off-our-hands-and-get-on-with-the-next-project kind of way. Removing Jim Crow laws off the books didn't end racism; the action just ended the Jim Crow laws and minimized that type of overt racism. The closing of all coal-fired power plants in the US would most likely lead to cleaner air, but what happens to states whose economies are largely based on extracting fossil fuels? Will the fairly widespread acceptance of the Common Core State Standards be enough to make a positive change in public education, or does such a change also rely on delivery of instruction, equity in funding, and other sociocultural factors (Loveless, 2012)?

If complexity does not lend itself to solutions, it does lend itself to challenge and engagement. Earlier on, we indicated that we choose to look at the cosmos of our classrooms with eyes of wonder and invited you to remember with us why the work we do is so lively, why working with young people is such an honor, and why, with stakes so high, we can't consider doing less. Complexity alone should not be daunting; it's entering that complex context with a lack of belief in process and no tools for dialoguing through it that appears futile.

If decisions we make within complex contexts like classrooms and schools only alter the current tack under which we sail and will most likely introduce new elements of concern to our context, then we who work within those contexts need to be ever mindful of and ever engaged with those shifting landscapes, both externally and internally. In particular we need to be alert for moments of wobble, those first indications that change is in the offing and we can either help steer the direction of that change or be at the mercy of whichever ways the winds blow. In the next chapter, we argue that reading, writing, speaking, and listening in engaged ways offer a powerful means for students and teachers to minimize the drift and maximize the ability to change course with intention, yet in response to the shifting context.

References

Altman, I. (2016). Ian's story. In B. Fecho, M. Falter, and X. Hong (Eds.) *Teaching outside the box but inside the standards: Making room for dialogue* (pp. 45–64). New York: Teachers College Press.

Bakhtin, M. (1981). *The dialogic imagination: Four essays by M. M. Bakhtin.* C. Emerson and M. Holquist, Trans. Austin, TX: U of Texas Press. (Original work published 1975.)

Bakhtin, M. (1984). *Rabelais and his world.* Helene Iswolsky, Trans. Bloomington, IN: U of Indiana Press. (Original work published 1965.)

Bakhtin, M. (1986). *Speech genres & other late essays.* V. W. McGee, Trans. Austen, TX: U of Texas Press.

Bakhtin, M. M., and Medvedev, P. N. (1978). *The formal method in literary scholarship: A critical introduction to sociological poetics.* Albert J. Wehrle, Trans. Cambridge, MA: Harvard University Press.

Bateson, M. C. (2010). *Composing a further life: The age of active wisdom.* New York: Vintage Books.

Clifton, J., and Sigoloff, J. (2013). Writing as dialogue across difference: Inventing genres to support deliberative democracy. *English Journal* 103(2), 73–84.

Cochran-Smith, M., and Lytle, S. L. (2009). *Inquiry as stance: Practitioner research for the next generation.* New York: Teachers College Press.

Dean, A. (2016). Angela's story. In B. Fecho, M. Falter, and X. Hong (Eds.) *Teaching outside the box but inside the standards: Making room for dialogue* (pp. 65–84). New York: Teachers College Press.

de Bono, E. (2015). *Lateral thinking: Creativity step by step.* New York: Harper Colophon.

Diaz, T. (2015). Arizona gets schooled: Update on ban of Mexican American studies #MayaVsAZ. *Huffington Post.* Retrieved from http://www.huffingtonpost.com/tonydiaz/discrimination-is-the-onl_b_7783704.html

Emerson, C. (1981). The outer world and inner speech: Bakhtin, Vygotsky, and the internalization of language. In G. S. Morson (Ed.) *Bakhtin: Essays and dialogues on his work.* Chicago: The University of Chicago Press.

Hacking, I. (2007). Kinds of people: Moving targets. *British Academy Lecture* 11 April 2006.

Hanes, S. (2013). Immigration: Assimilation and the measure of an American. *Christian Science Monitor.* Retrieved from http://www.csmonitor.com/USA/Society/2013/0707/Immigration-Assimilation and-the-measure-of-an-American

Hermans, H., and Hermans-Konopka, A. (2010). *Dialogical self theory: Positioning and counter-positioning in a globalizing society.* Cambridge: Cambridge UP.

La Vecchia-Mikkola, V. (2011). A tale of two cities: Iraqis' accounts of home and belonging in the city of Helsinki and in the city of Rome. In F. Eckardt, and J Eade (Eds.) *Ethnically diverse city.* Berlin: BWV—Berliner Wissenschafts-Verlag.

Loveless, T. (2012). The 2012 Brown Center report on American education: How well are American students learning: With sections on predicting the effect of the Common Core State Standards, achievement gaps on the two NAEP tests, and misinterpreting international test scores. Retrieved from www.brookings.edu/~/media/newsletters/0216_brown_education_loveless.pdf

Maguire, M. H., and Graves, B. (2001). Speaking personalities in primary school children's L2 writing. *TESOL Quarterly* 35(4), 561–593.

Morris, P. (1994). *The Bakhtin reader: Selected writings of Bakhtin, Medvedev, Voloshinov.* London: Edward Arnold.

North, D. S. (2009). The immigrant paradox. The stalled progress of recent immigrants' children. Retrieved from http://cis.org/ImmigrantParadox

Paris, D. (2012). Become history: Learning from identity texts and youth activism in the wake of Arizona SB1070. *International Journal of Multicultural Education* 14(2), 1–13.

Pew Study Social Trends (2013). Second-generation Americans: A Portrait of the adult children of immigrants. Retrieved from http://www.pewsocialtrends.org/2013/02/07/second-generation-americans/

Pinnow, R. J. (2015). A Patriot is respectful: (Re-) Examining the architecture of ideology in educational contexts. In P. Trifonas (Ed.) *International Handbook of Semiotics* (pp. 1249–1269). New York, NY: Springer.

Pope, D. (2003). *Doing school: How we are creating a generation of stressed-out, materialistic, and miseducated students.* New Haven, CT: Yale UP.

Schön, D. (1984). *The reflective practitioner: How professionals think in action.* New York: Basic Books.

Skerry, P. (2000). Do we really want immigrants to assimilate? Retrieved from http://www.brookings.edu/research/articles/2000/03/immigration-skerry

Warner, M. (2002). *Publics and counterpublics.* New York: Zone Books.

Young, I. M. (1996). Communication and the other: Beyond deliberative democracy. In S. Benhabib (Ed.) *Democracy and difference: Contesting the boundaries of the political* (pp. 120–136). Princeton, NJ: Princeton UP.

Young, I. M. (1997). *Intersecting voices: Dilemmas of gender, political philosophy and policy.* Princeton, NJ: Princeton UP.

Young, I. M. (2002). *Inclusion and democracy.* Oxford: Oxford UP.

Young, I. M. (2011). *Justice and the politics of difference.* Princeton, NJ: Princeton UP.

3

LITERACIES, LEARNING, CULTURES, AND THE DIALOGICAL SELF

Mahin, an Arab American and, at the time, a pre-service teacher, wrote about a discussion she witnessed in a local classroom in Missouri (rendered here as written):

> The students in a combined AP U.S History and English class, were all juniors, and most were white. There were probably about three Black students, and three Asians in the group of almost forty students. All semester long snippets of conversation could be heard from one black girl, in particular, that applied to her situation as a student of color, in an AP class:
>
> - White people are surprised that my parents push me to get good grades, as if grades are not a priority to black parents!
> - There are only three black people in this class, yet we're all over the school. How does that even happen? There has to be smarter black kids in our school than just us!
>   Black people totally would get February to celebrate Black History month, it's the shortest month, and the nastiest weather-wise…
>
> Later in the semester—on the day the class started talking about the N-word, slavery, Huck Finn, and the racially charged issues within the novel—was the day all the students of color became a lot more vocal. The teacher was giving a lesson about who should and shouldn't say the N-word, and white students were all looking down and not talking.

Teacher (after explaining her personal views about saying the N-word): *"I'm going to read a paragraph and say the word; do you have anything to say before I read?"*
White students (avoiding eye contact): ⋆*silence*⋆

Teacher (after reading aloud N____ from a paragraph in Huck Finn): *"What are your thoughts? How does this language make you feel?"*

Student of Color 1 (sighing): *"You know I'm not gonna hate you guys if you have an opinion about the word N_____."*

Other students: *★nervous laughs★*

★Silence★

Teacher (obviously turning to a student of color): *"What are your thoughts?"*

Student of Color 1 (sighing heavily): *"You know, every time we talk about slavery or the n-word, or racism all you teachers do is look to the people of color in the room to say something, like no one else has anything to say."* (Looks around, counting all the black kids.) *"There's three of us in this room. And 20 more white people that could say something. I wasn't a slave. I wasn't segregated. I don't want people calling me a N____ unless it's my black friends or family, but no one's calling me that in a bad way, at least to my face. Just because I'm black doesn't mean I have something profound to say about all of this. I mean I have an opinion, and an inside look at racism today, but surely you can call on someone else, and not just the black kid just because we're talking about black issues. We don't just call on Native Americans when we're talking about their issues."*

Teacher (taken aback): *"Those are some really interesting thoughts."*

Student of Color 2: *"I'm like 1/4 black, and a lot of people think I'm Hispanic. And they ask me about immigration and drug wars and stuff, and I don't know what to say. I agree with her. I feel like teachers and other students expect us to talk about the racial issues because it's hard for them to, because they're white and other students too. I won't be offended if people have an opinion. But just having people avoid the topic and the word all together, seems stupid. I've been called N_____ before, and obviously this novel still kind of relates to today, but we should all be able to have a discussion. Not just the black kids."*

Mahin said she chose to dramatize this critical incident (Clifton & Sigoloff, 2013) to deliberate with other new teachers about this kind of situation and possibilities for engaging each other differently because, as an Arab American, she has had similar experiences. She remembers teachers and others turning to her first when discussing issues like the Iraq War, 9/11, and Arab Spring, "as if my ethnicity gives me more of an insight into these issues than anything else. Perhaps it does. It isn't that I don't find an interest in topics about other Arabs and Arab countries, but when I'm constantly being put at the center of these conversations and issues, it can be annoying, disheartening, and even a little insensitive."

Like Mahin, the young African-American women in the class were frustrated with, yet again, having to "represent the race" (Mack, 2012). The young woman who spoke up is rightly angry by the limited ways others—in this case her White teacher and her White classmates—constitute Black experience, Black identity, her Black self. They have constructed her as "the representative woman," in some way supposing that she can somehow represent all of African-American experience to them in a way they will understand and that an entire people can be encapsulated in a singular self, as a "type." This historical I-position of a race representative has deep roots, stemming from what Kenneth Mack calls an "enduring paradox" of race relations, a paradox relevant to the American cultural imaginary and to our discussion about dialogical selves:

> From their beginnings, Americans inhabited a country composed of distinct racial, ethnic, and religious groups that somehow constituted a unified nation—an idea that, for some, is encapsulated in the historic national motto, e pluribus unum. Just as assuredly, since the time of the nation's founding Americans have imagined that certain minority groups fit uneasily, or perhaps not at all, into the national whole. Among the most prominent of these groups have been African Americans, and what has connected this particular minority group to the larger nation has been its representatives— those who claimed to speak for, stand in for, and advocate for the interests of the larger group.
>
> *(Mack, 2012, p. 4)*

Imagining American national identity in terms of a singular national "self" contributes to insider–outsider binaries; similar binaries are constructed when an individual's self is imagined as singular and monologic. In a singular individual or cultural self, identities and positions that somehow "fit uneasily" are silenced, pushed aside, not considered, not integrated. In the case of a national "self," casting people to the margins puts the burden of constructing dialogue on those in the margins and creates a need for marginalized representatives capable of fitting in enough that those who see themselves as part of the singular national self will listen. In US history, these representatives—lawyers, bankers, teachers, preachers, civil rights activists—were people often "caught between the needs and desires of the larger, White-dominated culture, and those of their own racial group, and there was no simple way out of that dilemma" (Mack, 2012) that demands both authenticity and exceptionalism.

In the classroom discussion about Huck Finn, the White teacher and White classmates, whether they realize it or not, were reproducing an I-position for the youth of color—as "race representatives." The African-American young woman resisted the very notion of being a "representative" as an option. She and other students of color in the class expressed frustration with the ways people have essentialized them based on an I-position they both contest and resent. The African-American young woman also marked the predictable and patterned way White teachers and classmates often constitute themselves as monologic singular selves—a position derived from a singular monologic national "self" that is some-how unified in its silence and unresponsiveness, insulated from and dumbfounded by Black experience and Black history.

In response, the youth of color tried to historicize themselves and differently contextualize and humanize themselves while also indicting the teacher and their peers for constructing youth of color as "representative" and positioning them simultaneously as monologic insiders of Black culture and monologic outsiders of

(White) American culture. The youth who spoke up in class, and Mahin who wrote about them, expressed the limits they experience of seeing the self only or primarily in terms of identity politics and expressed a need for much more dialogical literacy practices that might also call on and foster more dialogical selves.

Further they noted that essentializing an I-position as "representative" is neither helpful nor likely accurate. Although the argument is more implicit than explicit, they are positing that they have more to offer the class than a perspective based solely on race or ethnicity. Like everyone else in the class, they are in dialogue with a range of I-positions and cultural experiences that move them far beyond any monological stance. Their argument also implies that although the context of the class, or discussions of Huck Finn, may frequently position the three Black students along lines of race, such positioning in no way means that they necessarily share the same perspectives on race, racism, or any issue. Nor do they see their views on race and racism as any more valid or important than those of others in the class.

CONNECTING TO PRACTICE

Young people call on and leverage multiple literacies—ways of doing, talking, dressing, being, believing, writing, reading, designing, joking, and so on (Gee, 1991)—to enact socially situated identities with others. School-based literacies—those practices primarily taught, modeled, and enacted in relation to school—are sometimes the only literacies talked about, taught, or valued in schools. And yet, young people need to learn to call on and leverage a whole host of other literacy practices, in and out of school. Further, because literacies are also political—that is, differently connected to power relations—young people also need to be able to determine which literacies others expect in certain situations, how to enact those literacies wisely and well, what is at stake in enacting those literacies—what stands to be gained or lost and to what degree, and when and how those literacies—the practices and the relationships they construct—can be revised and transformed. Here, we offer two approaches.

Researching Their Own Lives and Literacies

In and out of school, young people are calling on literacy practices to read social situations and to enact cultural identities with others. Rather than teaching literacies in prescriptive ways, we suggest constructing a shared inquiry into these literacies with youth documenting and theorizing the range of literacies they already perform in sophisticated and savvy ways. In the same way that young people might call on a host of languages in a single

Gee
-multiple
literacies

repertoire (Alvarez, 2014; García & Wei, 2014; Lu & Horner, 2016), young people also have available to them—as a single repertoire—literacies that support their multiple selves-in-dialogue.

A single youth might, for example, enact with varying degrees of insider expertise any combination of these situated literacies: *hip-hop literacies*, like hush mode or battlin (Alim, 2004); *gaming literacies*, like those associated with Minecraft or World of Warcraft (Gee, 2003; Steinkuehler, 2008); *multilingual literacies*, like language sharing (Paris, 2013), translanguaging (Alvarez, 2014; Garcia & Flores, 2015; Lu & Horner, 2016), multimodal translation (Gonzalez, 2015), and code-switching (Young et al., 2014); *rural literacies*, like understanding local food production, the "farm crisis," and Farm Aid (Donehower, Hogg, & Schell, 2007; Green & Corbett, 2013; Azano, 2015); *indigenous and mestizo literacies*, like performing the dances of each season, knowing the sacred values of certain animals, recognizing trickster characters, reading and writing pictographs and syllabaries, hiding in plain sight, knowing how to grow different varieties of corn or how to dig and maintain an acequia (Powell, 2014; Cushman, 2013; Baca, 2008; Long, Jarvis, & Deerheart Raymond, 2013; San Pedro, 2015); *urban literacies*, like recognizing impacts of gentrification (Kinloch, 2009), valuing "street survivors" (Kinloch, 2009), and producing multimodal identity texts (Paris, 2010; Kirkland, 2009; Morrell et al., 2013); *athlete literacies*, like how to read a playbook or a strength training workout or how to read a change in defense on the court; *Muslim literacies*, like when and how to wear a hijab, how to read the Koran, and which way to turn to face Mecca; *drama literacies*, like how to do improv or staged fighting (Edmiston, 2013); or *migrant literacies*, like keeping vaccination records and work papers or knowing migratory patterns that follow different harvest times and crop locations (Purcell-Gates, 2013).

Documenting these and then naming and describing particular practices *and* the situated decision-making that youth must exercise to know when and how to enact these practices constructs movement across these literacies as a dialogical space and makes visible a self-in-dialogue. Taking a critical approach to make sense of the ways others perceive those literacies and what Is at stake in the situated decision-making youth do creates a more expansive dialogue about *making up people* and *looping back,* and demonstrates an ongoing need for *self-agreement, self-consultancy, self-conflict,* and *self-critique.*

Inventing Alternative Literacies

Taking a critical approach to researching literacies also recognizes the possible limitations of current literacies to reach across or transform moments when youth most experience literacies, cultures, and identities in conflict.

In these cases—like the one Mahin documents—alternative literacies (Higgins, Long, & Flower, 2006) are needed that offer new or hybrid practices to resist the ways some literacies are stigmatized, to create at least a temporary shared We-ness, to construct more just self/other relations, and to forge a way forward together.

In the classroom discussion about Huck Finn, for example, the young African-American woman is recognizing the limitations of current literacy practices related to classroom conversations about race. Together, they might consider other possible alternatives. One might be to ask each person in the room to write down their initial thoughts, and especially their worries, related to having a discussion about race. Maybe the teacher collects them all and reads each one anonymously while a student writes a list of shared worries. Then, perhaps they do the same thing with their hopes for a discussion about race.

But there are other alternatives. Maybe they determine a shared purpose for talking about historical or current, fictionalized or nonfiction depictions of race relations—what is it they want to better understand? Maybe they create some ground rules for these discussions that invite everyone to participate, that make space for changes in thought or reasoning, that allow room for someone to mis-speak, that recognize the need to process feelings and experiences along with thoughts and logics, that invite alternative readings of a situation, that aim to test ideas while sustaining cultures and dignity, and that create practices of *self-agreement, self-consultancy, self-conflict, self-critique,* and other ways of engaging in self-dialogue. Perhaps, they also talk about other possible practices, like students being able to suggest a think–pair–share when they need time to gather their thoughts or want to test their ideas with a friend first; that might have been useful in response to the teacher's question about reading the N-word in Huck Finn: *"What are your thoughts? How does this language make you feel?"* Or they might interview youth across campus about their experiences of race relations and make sense of those different experiences in relation to Huck Finn or Pedro or Trayvon Martin or Sandra Bland or Ersula Ore or …

None of these possibilities—a shared purpose, ground rules, alternative practices—*guarantee* productive dialogue or more just relations. Just as we are always doing, being, and becoming, so, too, are our literacies—our ways of dialoguing and using texts, our ways of being and doing together—always in process, always in need of inventing and reinventing.

We have already discussed Adichie's (2009) warning about the danger of a single story, of how seeing someone or some group or some culture through a single lens or based on a finite set of actions results too often in constricted and repressive understandings. In a more recent TED talk, Taiye Selasie (2015) argued that we shouldn't ask where people are from, we instead should ask where are they local. According to Selasie, to ask where someone is from is to, in many ways, essentialize and severely confine your understanding of who they have been, who they are being, and who they are becoming. She instead argued that by asking where acquaintances are local, we provide an opening for them to share a range of contexts that have transacted with their dialogical selves.

We need only go as far as our own lives for an example. If you asked Bob where he was from, with the expectation of him responding with his place of birth, his answer—Reading, Pennsylvania—would offer small insight into the complexity of experience that 60 plus years have garnered. Additionally, much of your assessment would be based upon single stories of what you knew about people who grow up in small cities or who grow up in Pennsylvania or who grow up in the US northeast. Similarly, to ask the same of Jen would let you know that she grew up in the South—in Savannah, Georgia, to be exact—but any caricatured, or even nostalgic, notions of the South that might come to mind would tell you little about Jen as a person or about her complex and layered histories with Savannah or with the South.

In both cases, the sense of being local in many places gives greater insight into the lived experiences of the two of us. Philadelphia; Athens, Georgia; New York City; Adelaide, Australia are but a few places where Bob has spent enough time to have a sense of self in and local to. As for Jen, Savannah and Cartersville, Georgia; Fort Meade, Maryland; Beijing; and Phoenix, Arizona along with several other places have informed the many ways she might experience a local self. Both of us also feel local at universities, in high schools, at literacy conferences and other shared educational settings. Each of these contexts of locality has transacted with our many I-positions and continues those transactions as we move through other and diverse localities.

Shifting back to the students Mahin observed in class, they, too, have more than a single story to be embraced and hail from multiple localities. Within the classroom event described earlier, they are calling on those multiple perspectives and localities in order to urge their peers and teachers of other cultures and identities to think together with them. Importantly, they want their peers and teachers to offer their White or Arab or Native American selves *as well as* other parts of their selves. They seem to invite their peers to engage tough questions as student-scholars, as caring and concerned citizens, and as complex and diverse people. They are raising questions of what we can and should do with differences within and across selves. This exchange also raises questions and possibilities for thinking about literacies capable of valuing differences and supporting the ideological becoming of dialogical selves.

Literacies and Dialogical Selves

While we start this chapter with a scene in a classroom centered on a canonical novel, we will frame our discussion of literacies much more broadly and expansively. Drawing on the work of New Literacy Studies scholars (Gee, 1991; Street, 1995),

New Lit Studies scholars

we see literacy not as a set of discrete skills but as social practices that vary across time and space, taking different forms and having different consequences. As the uses and meanings of isolated literacy events and culturally or institutionally embedded literacy practices vary across different cultural and social contexts, literacy is not a singular thing but is instead multiple. The social practices surrounding the ways texts of all kinds are used in one classroom are quite different from another, and the social practices around the ways youth use texts in school may be quite different from those around playing video games online with friends and strangers or repairing a mountain bike or prepping for a role in a play or applying for college.

If a person wants to be part of cultures or groups who do X, that person must learn the social practices of that group in ways that are recognizable and valued by that group, whether these social practices are those of a particular job market or a particular educational context or a particular group of activist hackers. These multiple literacies are, then, deeply tied to taking on particular identities and becoming "certain kinds of people" (Hacking, 2007). And yet, the social practices, assumptions, and values of one culture or group or identity do not necessarily transfer to those of another. Sometimes different literacies may fit well together, but often a person has to "leave"—perhaps only temporarily—one set of specialized social practices in order to acquire or leverage another. For example, our continued acquisition of standard edited English has always been in dialogue with our primary discourses and, at times, one or the other may rise to the surface. However, some discourses, including standard edited English, may include values and practices that are so different from another discourse a person commands that participation in that second (or third, or fourth, or fifth …) discourse requires a kind of setting aside of another discourse, even though neither is ever gone. In this kind of "exchange," some value-laden practices may be gained and others lost or set aside, which constructs learning multiple discourses as a deeply personal project.

Take, for instance, a Tigua graduate student in environmental science working with Tigua elders, university faculty, and the National Park Service who sought to retell the story of the Chamizal Treaty of 1963, a treaty between Mexico and the US that concretized the Rio Grande and solidified the US–Mexico border. This treaty also robbed the Tigua of water, a living spiritual entity central to their ceremonies and lifeways, and diverted the river from their lands, making their land impossible to farm. When the Tigua student asked her mentors about studying the river's changes over time and their impact on her people, her university mentors told her she could not include the stories of her people; instead, her research and writing must focus strictly on the hard science of the river's changes.

While these disciplinary distinctions are common in schools, Linda Smith (1999) argued, referring to the work of Frantz Fanon and others, that these divisions are contemporary legacies of imperialism disconnecting colonized peoples from their histories and systematically fragmenting the indigenous world with "bones, mummies, and skulls to museums, art work to private collectors, languages to linguistics, 'customs' to anthropologists, beliefs and behaviors to psychologists" (p. 28). That this

Tigua scientist must segment and siphon off ways of knowing most dear to her, that she is advised by the most compassionate and caring researchers she can find to set aside the lifeblood of the river and of her people, and that she is told that these things have no place in science or in her writing creates not just a border between one kind of knowledge and another, one way of being and another; it creates a border within her as well, to separate her identity as an indigenous woman from her identity as a scientist.

Literacies, then, are always contested, both their meanings and their practices. Particular versions are always ideological since they are always rooted in a particular worldview (Gee, 1991; Besnier & Street, 1994) and embedded with assumptions and power relations as the social practices of particular literacies are situated within cultures and within structures of power (Street, 1995). Context and ideological struggle are, then, at the center of literacy practices and literacy instruction. The text itself is less important than what people are doing with a text, shaping reading and writing to their purposes. Further, what people are doing with a text is seldom, if ever, in isolation; thus, literacy is primarily a form of social participation, and literacy learning is primarily a form of socialization (Brandt & Clinton, 2002).

Yet, as we have stated earlier and will continue to expand throughout this book, individuals must navigate the multiple ways they are being socialized through cultural literate practices, practices that are at times overlapping or at odds with a person's other cultures and other literate practices. For some students, school can be one site where literate practices are a site of personal turmoil. Certainly social, economic, and political forces collude to centripetally constrict and limit modes of language use and expression. Likewise, the banking model of literacy education that Freire (1970) criticized—one that views students as receptacles for knowledge deposits made by teachers—is much too present in too many educational systems. The tendency to view language in narrow and decontextualized ways spills over into education, prompting many policymakers to see teaching and learning similarly narrow and decontextualized, more about discrete and seemingly neutral skills than cultural and ideological ways of making meaning with others.

Language users aren't, however, totally at the mercy of such tensions. Each of us, whether consciously or subconsciously, has some ken that alongside "centralization and unification, the uninterrupted processes of decentralization and disunification go forward" (Bakhtin, 1981, p. 272). Some of this decentralization is powered by social and historical tensions, but much of it comes out of an individual's needs to make language something intimately reflective of themselves. Ideas we share through language may go out with the still visible fingerprints of others to whom we've responded, but our fingerprints sit atop those, smudge and blur them, render them apparent, but less clear. As we continue through this chapter, our intent is to play with these ideas touched on to this point, the better to understand how our literacies transact with how we learn in the context of our multiple cultures.

Connecting Bakhtin, Literacy, and the Dialogical Self

Building on the discussion that ended the previous section, we argue that when we teach children to read and write, we are often teaching them to accept and work within a fairly unified code. This unification, up to a point, is necessary and useful. In order for large numbers of people to communicate, Bakhtin (1981) argued, we need centripetal forces acting on the language to center and unify it. Mass communication depends on such unification. For example, when Bob gave a talk at a conference in South Korea, he knew that the audience was indulging his inability to speak Korean or Hangul by their agreeing to experience the talk in English. For that event, there was no other way, even though he suspected that the more subtle aspects of his presentation might be lost on those less fluent in English. Or consider if we had made a decision to write the text of this book in *flash*, an argot of gangs and newsboys in nineteenth-century New York (see novels by Lindsay Faye). In doing so, we most likely would have severely cut our readership. Even conventions in punctuation are tools for writers and signals for readers that ease fluency, comprehension, and interpretation, despite such conventions remaining in ever-evolving flux. Unification of language allows greater numbers of people to share ideas, revelations, concerns, ideologies, and all else we construct through language.

However, unification can be overdone, turning language and meaning constructed through language to stone, which is why oppressive regimes and governments obsessed with nationalism almost always enact measures that constrict language use and the flow of information across media. Google being banned from China, English-only movements in the US, attempts by the *Académie Française* to provide French equivalents for English words like *software* and *email*, arrests of journalists in Egypt after the Arab Spring, and initiatives to limit what we mean by the term *marriage* despite evolving social contexts are all examples of ways that the centered unification of language becomes constrictive and supportive of oppression. Think about it: if *freedom* were to mean only the absence of restraint, would people continue to put their lives in danger for it?

Connecting to our experiences with international conferences where the *lingua franca*, the accepted common language, is English, we native speakers frequently have a distinct advantage over those whose first language is other than English. We have often watched bright and vivacious scholars at a conference exuberantly converse in their language of birth during a coffee break only to later present a halting, discontinuous talk as they attempted to navigate in a language with which they were neither comfortable nor practiced—something neither of us would be able to do even a third as well if we had to present in another language. Both of us are also well aware that it is far easier for us to be at a kimchi shop in Seoul and find a Korean somewhat conversant in English than it is for a Korean scholar visiting the US to find an American deli clerk even minimally conversant in Korean. Such is the current predominance of English that those of us who grew up using the language frequently aren't aware of the privilege it accords us globally. But language tides shift. If China or Japan or Brazil or Germany (or whomever) were to become a large global economic, political, and social power, how soon will it be when international scholars need to learn to present in Mandarin or Japanese or Portuguese or German or …?

For it is often these power structures of globalization that drive greater conformity of language use. One trend that global linguists are tracking is how such conformity crowds out other languages. Even using adjusted figures that somewhat lessen the direness of earlier reports, the website of the Rosetta Project indicated that we are losing languages at a rapid, and perhaps even alarming rate. Highlighting work done through the Endangered Languages Catalog (ELCat) of the University of Hawai'i at Manoa and Eastern Michigan University, the website reported that nearly 3,200 languages are endangered with extinction, and that the world loses a language at the rate of one every three months. Assuming that rate doesn't accelerate—which it is more likely to do than slacken—that would be 340 languages lost over the rest of this century. Regional dialects are also being swept aside, as geographical barriers that once limited the range of contact that locals had with groups beyond a mountain or across a river are easily penetrated by digital means.

Those of us who still retain a living language may wonder what the fuss is about, but, then, we're not the ones losing the words, the meanings, the histories, the cultures that are tied to a language and its unique forms of expression. We've all heard of words with no direct English translation (e.g., *fernweh*, a German word for feeling homesick for a place you've never been or the Japanese *tsundoku*, having a collection of books that you bought, but have never read). When we push too hard for conformity, in addition to actual languages, we lose the ability to express the interesting nuances, experiences, and ideologies that language cultures create.

However, all is not gloom of night regarding language use. Simultaneously with the centripetal tug toward center, Bakhtin (1981) continued, centrifugal forces direct languages away from center. Cultural groups and individuals put their own meanings and spin on words. A facile example is how regional groups in the US create a plural form of the pronoun *you*. If someone were to look toward a class of students and say, "You should leave," it would be unclear if she meant one, some, or all. To counter this ambiguity, where Bob grew up near Philadelphia, they said, "Yous" and across the state they said, "You'uns," while in Georgia, one of Jen's locales, they said "Y'all." In each case, attempts were being made locally to fill a language gap. Despite the reluctance of social, political, and economic power structures to relent and construct a plural *you*—and, in fact, these power structures often demean those who use a plural you—many of us continue to find ways to introduce such usage into our daily speech.

Frequently, if not always, the ways we encounter language at cultural boundaries result in interesting combinations and reconfigurations of language that illustrate and remind us that languages live and are dynamic. Bakhtin (1981) noted what he termed stratification in language and, although we are less comfortable with the value-laden connotations of that term (e.g., language X is superior to language Y)—we join him in the celebratory, carnivalesque tone (1981, 1984) with which he discussed it. Professions have their jargon. Generations have their slang. Regions have their words that are place specific. Studies of hip-hop culture and learning (Alim, 2006; Jocson, 2008; Kirkland, 2008; Meacham, Anderson, & Correa, 2013; Morrell & Duncan-Andrade, 2002) have shown how immersion in the flux, the rhythms, the possibilities of language generates not only art, literature, music, and entrepreneurship, but also an ever shifting stream of word usage and connotation. Among communities where English is a second or even third language, hybrids—or as some would theorize, whole new languages (Alvarez, 2014; García & Wei, 2014; Lu & Horner, 2016)—like Spanglish, Chinglish, and Konglish proliferate. Mixing English terms and grammar with Spanish, Chinese, and Korean respectively—usually in the same utterance—translanguaging represents the complex needs and expectations of people crossing language and cultural boundaries, sometimes by force, sometimes out of pragmatism, sometimes by choice.

A colleague of Bakhtin, Valentin Vološinov (1929–1986), made a number of interesting insights about language that have resonance in this discussion. To start, he echoed Bakhtin by stating that meaning is determined by context, but built on that notion by arguing that "there are as many meanings of a word as there are contexts of its usage" (p. 79), that is to say an infinite number of meanings. Additionally, contexts are not separate with crisp edges and defined borders, but remain in "constant tension, or incessant interaction and conflict" (p. 80) with each other. Vološinov also dismissed the idea that language is handed down from generation to generation, as if it were on tablets inscribed by the word of a god. Instead, language "endures as a continuous process of becoming" (p. 81). We, as users of language, continue to exert opposite pressure on society's center-ing pull by immersing language in use through a range of contexts. In doing so, individual understandings are always being created.

If we were to market a Vološinov t-shirt—yes, wouldn't that be a big seller—we'd put his picture on the front and, across our shoulders, we'd have "expression organizes experience" (Vološinov, 1986, p. 85). We will come back to this idea later in the chapter, but, for now, just consider the ramifications of that statement. Until we put experience into language of some form, it remains amorphous and grows in its ineffability. Without expression—a word spoken, a line drawn, a sentence written, a gesture made—it is difficult, if not altogether impossible to construct meaning from our daily experiences across a multitude of contexts. And certainly completely impossible to convey thought to another. By expressing a thought—always in response to self and other—we seek to make sense, to construct meaning, to provoke understanding of what happens to us and how we happen to others. Our lives, that of our families and closest friends, the lives of the people with whom we share cultures, the teeming mass of organisms that we

[handwritten annotations: "language shifts naturally — cunning it is a way to try to control who is in power . knows the lay b/c lang"]

contemporaneously, but temporarily share this planet, galaxy, and universe with are connected through an ongoing and complex weave of response.

Through the individualizing centrifugal process, meaning and usage are no longer centrally controlled. Language users are free to invent, play, nuance, complicate, shift, nudge, and basically keep the language in motion, breathing, developing, evolving. However, if languages skew too far toward individualism, communication suffers. If we were to ask that Korean audience Bob addressed to take a few minutes to *schmooze*, well who knows what we might see occurring. Would it fadge as a lay if we blew the gab that some of our readers are dimber dead rabbits? It might do (fadge) as a kind of rascality (lay) if you understood *flash* and grasped that we confessed (blew the gab) that some of our readers were handsome and athletic (dimber dead rabbits). In fact, one of the main points of argots like flash and the slang developed by any number of cultures is to exclude, to limit the in-crowd. We maintain that the minute middle-aged adults begin adopting slang developed by youth culture is the minute that youth culture starts to drop those words (witness, from a few years back, *my bad*, or more recently, the change from *lol* to *haha* to emojis in textspeak) (Research at Facebook, 2015).

In a like manner, an insistence on rigid observation of standard edited English (SEE) is also a way to exclude, and such exclusion frequently comes at the price of limiting or even barring access to power venues and not just language access. Unless we, as language scholars of certain ages, imagine a career shift into hip-hop or want to focus on the linguistics of that evolving culture or aim to join with young people to understand and value the resonance they feel with the poetry and history of that culture of resistance, it harms us little to not have access to it. However, a creative and insightful young man from a working-class neighborhood who might wish to penetrate mainstream law firms will be expected by the vast majority of potential employers to master the verb agreement rules of SEE, no matter what it might mean for how he constructs his sense of self through his primary discourse. *[handwritten: power w/in languages]*

Although teachers and educational researchers have, in the past, made the case that we need to teach students how to switch language codes to meet the constraints of varying contexts, doing so—due to issues connected to identity, history, and even current events—is far more complex than we in language education make it sound. Bob's (Fecho, 2004) work in this area showed how the working class and working poor Black students he taught in Philadelphia realized politically and pragmatically that if they wanted to continue their education and/or land jobs outside the borders of their community, that they would need to become proficient with SEE. That noted, most reluctantly accepted this expectation because such proficiency often conflicted with the identities they were constructing and too closely aligned them with power structures that had long held them in opposition. Though the studies that led to this work are now over a decade old, the understandings derived from them remain relevant in too many cases.

Learning within Tensions

Ultimately, it's the tension between social forces seeking to unify language and more individual forces seeking to personalize language that creates a healthy and supportive context for dialogue. We need language to be unified and we need it to be individualized because both are conducive to the construction of new understandings. According to Bakhtin (1981), meaning is constructed in context and through response, going so far as to say that, regarding understanding and response, "one is impossible without the other" (p. 282). We use language—verbal, written, musical, visual, gestural, and so on—as a response and in the expectation of response.

When we endeavored to write this book, we were responding to many prior responses in our lives: articles and other pieces we've written earlier in our academic lives, articles and books we've read in the past; the blogs we shared with each other that indicated where our work dovetailed and where it diverged; the suggestions of mentors to gather our ideas together into book form; images and ideas floating out of popular culture; stray comments by colleagues and students; every class we've ever taught and ever taken; and many more transactions that are far too numerous to mention. This web or mesh or rhizome of response enables us to establish "a series of complex interrelationships, consonances, and dissonances" with the words we encounter daily and the context within which we experience those words (Bakhtin, 1981, p. 282).

Then, when we have opportunities to respond across cultural boundaries, we open ourselves to new ways to perceive the worlds in which we live. Bakhtin spoke to the potency of such response and dialogue when he wrote that regarding culture, "outsideness is a most powerful factor in understanding" (1986, p. 7). His argument is that, as outsiders to a culture, we can help insiders to that culture raise questions that might not occur to them, but, at the same time, the other culture "responds to us by revealing to us new aspects and new semantic depths." Such cross-cultural encounters do not result in denigration of one culture by another, but instead, by inserting some wobble into the encounter, promote dialogue and lead to mutual enrichment.

In writing about the dialogical self, Hermans and Hermans-Konopka (2010) argued for the plurality of self and the ways facets of this plurality transact with external otherness. They argued that the self not only moves toward sameness and cohesion in identity, but at the same time seeks difference and diversity. Given that we construct identity through language, similar centering and decentering tensions are apparent. And, like language, our sense of self is most healthy when some equilibrium between these tensions is achieved and when our unifying sense of self is most dialogically open to our individualizing "outsideness."

One way to achieve this sense of equilibrium—of living in ways both united and multiple—is through self-reflection, a way of thinking about your ongoing construction of self through meta-positions (Hermans & Hermans-Konopka, 2010).

Meta positions

Such meta-positions allow you to step a little away from yourself, to look across I-positions, and to essentially take stock. In doing so, you can observe and construct new understandings that position us for future reflection. Perhaps you realize that quieter aspects of your personality have been neglected or ignored, or you draw links across various positions that heretofore were less obvious. Maybe you develop opportunities for greater dialogue across positions or become more aware of how certain positions may either hinder or fuel your ability to move in particular directions. Some meta-positions take a more ironic stance; others may gaze from a more worldly or more critical perspective. Ultimately, these meta-positions, like so much we've discussed in this text, are dependent on context and remain in flux. Metaphorically, Hermans and Hermans-Konopka (2010) likened meta-positions to a committee, a group in which different points of views are exchanged, where some voices may have more influence than others, but where the contributions of all members are welcomed.

Up to this point, we have been spinning a tale of complexity, one that argues that all people engage multiple contexts, that we all participate in a multiplicity of cultures, that we all move from one ideologically-saturated context to another, and that via response we remain in an ongoing process of meaning making through dialogue. All of that complexity comes together daily in classrooms across the US and, indeed, across the world. It might go without saying that such a high degree of complexity and flux can cause teachers and students high degrees of anxiety as they face the uncertainty that such conditions often prompt. Yet, dwelling within all that complexity and flux is a richness of experience, a treasure of possibility, and a garden of innovation. Literacy classrooms—places where students and teachers engage with and generate text—are uniquely situated for the kind of thoughtful meta-positioning that facilitates dialoguing through the uncertainty.

dwelling!

Implications for Teaching Reading and Writing

As we think about classrooms, the necessities of teaching reading and writing, and the complexities of doing so, it is apt to consider what the constructs of cultures, wobble, and the dialogical self bring to current and future instruction. We have never been ones to write about or argue for prescribed, discrete ways of teaching; rather, we strongly believe that teachers should leave themselves open to a range of approaches, but to also retain under construction a vibrant and thoughtful set of theories about teaching and learning. Therefore, what follows in this section is not a series of activities. The web is awash with such activities; some teachers, we hear, are adding substantially to their incomes via sales of them. Instead, we offer thoughts about how best to position yourself to inquire into and reflect on your classroom. The intent is for all who educate to be better able to shop for, invent, and adapt activities that will support their efforts to have themselves and their students transact across cultures through literacy practices.

We also firmly believe, as Frank Smith (2005) indicated, that all serious methods we've invented for teaching reading work; most students learn to read. However, what kinds of readers they'll turn out to be is what marks differences of significance among the methods. If we're satisfied with students being word callers or basic comprehenders of text, there are some narrow ways of conceiving and teaching reading that will most likely work. However, if our goal is to support students in becoming readers who interpret and generate complex text; who ask nuanced questions of what they read; who bring a critical stance to words, images, gestures, and sound; and who draw interesting and complex associations across experience and text, then a more inquiry-based and dialogical approach is needed, along with activities to match.

The theoretical stances we've laid out here, if developed into approaches and strategies within literacy classrooms, are designed to enable learners to see reading and writing in dialogical ways. Their intent is to help learners make sense of text within their cultural and individual contexts, but to continue to remain in dialogue and always be open to "the possibility of changing and even abandoning [their] prepared viewpoints and positions" (Bakhtin, 1986, p. 142). A learner who is taught to read and write through dialogical instruction should become a lifelong learner, a discerning reader, an open-minded maker of meaning, a self and other critical questioner, an inquirer into cultures, and an appreciator of nuance and complexity, to name just a few attributes that should result. If your intention as a teacher is to see more of such learners in the world, then please consider some of the following approaches.

Seek a Seamless Curriculum

What we mean by seamless is to view reading and writing activities—really all you do in your classroom—as connected. On one level that means creating lessons that help students to see that the reading and writing they do at the start of the week connects to other reading and writing at week's end. It also means that engaging with, for example, Anna Deavere Smith's *Fires in the Mirror* in September results in that engagement being raised again to the surface if transacting with *Spoon River Anthology* in December and/or *The House on Mango Street* in April. It means we need to stop teaching literature as one more text covered in the anthology or as something to be understood wholly unto itself as if it existed in a vacuum or as some revered icon forever to be knelt before or as some reified understanding to be learned rather than an opportunity for engagement, exploration, and interpretation. Accomplished independent readers make associations across all they read—sometimes overtly and sometimes tacitly—and those associations don't stop because they've closed the back cover or sent the file to the cloud. Those of us who labor in classrooms owe it to our students to provide multiple opportunities to overtly make similar associations, ones that spring from their engagement with the texts.

Seamlessness also involves having discussions that help students connect their work in class to those larger existential questions that compel us to examine self and other. What does it mean to be an adolescent? How do individuals and communities negotiate change? How does our burgeoning technology enhance and how does it lessen our lives? What does it mean to be a family? When we organize literature and response to literature around such questions rather than collecting what is to be read by genre, historical periods, or regions, we encourage all of us engaged in the study to see text as data to learn from and connect to other data sources. As a fairly frequent result, reading, writing, speaking, and listening become ways to engage the question from both personal and collaborative perspectives rather than assignments merely to be completed.

Encourage, Evoke, and Value Multiple Perspectives

If you strive toward seamlessness as we discussed above, then you'll create myriad opportunities for students and you to develop a range of perspectives on the questions you ask and the texts you engage. You almost won't be able to help yourself from doing so, not that you should or would. We ask, if directors George Cukor, Franco Zefferelli, and Baz Lurhmann can have such differing interpretations of *Romeo and Juliet*, why would we encourage learners not to? Haven't each brought a vision that was somehow influenced by the times in which they lived, the countries in which they were raised, the education they received, their individual life experiences, and their broad and individual range of sociocultural factors? Not doubting Shakespeare's talent for playing to his audience, he could never have imagined a transgender Korean American living in a rowhouse in twenty-first century Philadelphia reading or watching his play. Surely, she would have potential to bring unique understandings, as would the Black valedictorian at a private school, the devoutly Catholic Latina cheerleader in rural Georgia, the White Kansas farm boy anchoring the offensive line, or anyone else we could describe. As teachers in our own classrooms, we have found that creating opportunities for multiple perspectives makes classes as inventive and as interesting for teachers as it does for students. You're never quite sure what you'll learn next.

Have no doubt, however, that encouraging and valuing multiple perspectives is not the same as agreeing with all perspectives. If anything, expectations for vigorously and thoughtfully engaging text are upped when teachers allow for a range of perspectives. The intent is to recognize that all worldviews come from some set of lived experiences and bringing those experiences to the surface promotes richer and more nuanced understandings of the world. Students can give voice to opposing views, but no one has to agree with those views.

On the other hand, teachers do, we feel, have a responsibility to engage students in a dialogue that helps students to experience a moment of wobble, one that expects them to call their own views into question. The end result might be that students create an entirely new perspective or they might, instead, develop more informed arguments for the perspectives they hold or cultivate a range of understandings for future consideration. They could form momentary and fluctuating alliances of understanding with others in class. Students could find themselves more open to the perspectives of others without necessarily giving up their own. What no doubt will emerge is a richer mix, a think stew of ideas that otherwise would have remained tacit, hidden away, kept private. It's a stew into which all involved can dip their intellectual ladles.

Recognize Reading and Writing as Interpretive and Generative Acts

Most people have no difficulty in recognizing the generative aspects of writing; when we sit down with pen or keyboard, we produce a tangible product, something that can be seen. The same goes for any form of composition—music, art, photography, dance—something that can be perceived, often multimodally, is created. In the Stephen Sondheim (2011) musical, Sunday in the Park with George, the artist who created the pointillist painting, "A Sunday on La Grande Jatte" sings of "Finishing the hat. How you have to finish the hat. ... entering the world of the hat, reaching through the world of the hat like a window, from this world to that." Writing in dialogical ways is much like this description of artistic creativity. We consider, reflect, study, empathize, interpret and then generate text. Sondheim's artist, Georges Seurat, ends the song on two pithy lines: "Look, I made a hat. Where there never was a hat."

When any of us write, we are interpreting our contexts and generating text in order to construct meaning. We interpret what we hear, read, experience, sense and then we generate a response. But it's really no different in terms of reading. When any of us read anything, we generate a personal understanding of that text through interpretation. We, in effect, create a new text, a very personal one. However, unlike forms of composition, a tangible, hard and fast thing isn't always created when we read. Very often the forms of expression remain interior. However, that doesn't make them any less generative. As Louise Rosenblatt (1995) famously declared, there are as many interpretations of a text as there are readers of that text.

Taking the stance that reading and writing are generative and interpretive acts creates opportunities and space for the expression of a learner's many I-positions. It recognizes that everyone who enters a classroom brings the experiences of engaging across many cultures and invites them to explore the many texts of their lives through those many perspectives. In doing so, the classroom becomes an intentional ongoing dialogue in which individual stances, perspectives, and inter-pretations are explored, not with the intent of refutation or denigration, but in an effort to help all involved in the dialogue develop more complex understandings of themselves and the cultures in which they participate, as well as more complex understandings of culture of which they know little and understand less.

Embrace Complexity

People are complex multicultural beings engaging in complex multicultural contexts. We have stated such earlier, but it bears repeating. It's one thing to mouth a handy slogan and another to enact it. It's not enough in teaching to believe something is so. Teachers, really all in education, need to act in ways that reflect and realize what is believed. If teachers embrace that classrooms are sites of complexity and both teaching and learning are complex processes, then we suspect they will never again seek or allow others to foist on them simple contrivances that masquerade as "best practice." Instead, teachers will find ways to recognize wobble in their practices, to dialogue through the uncertainty, and then ready new questions to be asked and explored.

Moving Forward

To be true to our dialogical perspectives, we can go no further than this in our discussion of classroom approaches. What is written to this point is a framework with which you can dialogue and from which you can consider and invent how it might work in your classroom. It is our suspicion that parts of what we've discussed in this last section feel somewhat familiar to you, that you may have recognized aspects of your practice in our description. If so, it might just be a matter of you becoming more systematic and intentional about these ideas. Implementation wouldn't require a complete paradigm shift, but, rather, a flexible plan of action conceived from a reflection on how to narrow the gap between what you believe and what you do.

In trying to imagine how to shift your teaching in more dialogical ways and to mine the possibilities that a self-in-dialogue offers, we remind you that complexity doesn't indicate clear pathways to final solutions, but instead provides directions to be pursued and re-examined as contexts change. As such, you will need to remain in dialogue, not only with your students, but with your teaching context as well—the steady drizzle and even heavy downpour of changing policy, the supportive or nonsupportive moves of administrators, the often day-to-day and even hour-to-hour I-position fluctuations of maturing adolescents, the diverse needs of parents, the drifting *zeitgeist* of how teachers are viewed by politicians and the general public. You will do this even as you monitor the internal dialogue of sometimes dovetailing, sometimes contradicting I-positions. The benefit of taking this stance is to see your teaching practice as an organic and dynamic process over which you have more control than you might think and through which you can continue to evolve to the advantage of your students, yourself, and the many cultures within which you participate.

To motivate you, we leave you with what we hope is a thought-provoking quotation from Bakhtin (1986): "There can be neither a first nor last meaning; it always exists among other meanings as a link in the chain of meaning, which in its totality is the only thing that can be real" (p. 146). If the way you teach reading and writing in your classroom can only hew to that idea, you will have accomplished much.

References

Adichie, C. (2009, July). "Chimamanda Ngozi Adichie: The danger of a single story." [Video file]. Retrieved from https://www.ted.com/talks/chimamanda_adichie_the_danger_of_a_single_story?language=en

Alim, H. S. (2004). Hearing what's not said and missing what is: Black English in White public space. In C. Paulston and S. Keisling (Eds.) *Discourse and intercultural communication: The essential readings* (pp. 180–197). Malden, MA: Blackwell Publishers.

Alim, H. S. (2006). *Roc the mic right: The language of hip hop culture.* London & New York: Routledge.

Alvarez, S. (2014). Translanguaging *tareas*: Emergent bilingual youth as language brokers for homework in immigrant families. *Language Arts* 91(5), 326–339.

Azano, A. P. (2015). Addressing the rural context in literacies research: A call to action. *Journal of Adolescent & Adult Literacy* 59(3), 267–269.

Baca, D. (2008). *Mestiz@ scripts, digital migrations, and the territories of writing.* New York: Palgrave Macmillan.

Bakhtin, M. (1981). *The dialogic imagination: Four essays by M. M. Bakhtin.* C. Emerson and M. Holquist, Trans. Austen, TX: U of Texas Press. (Original work published 1975.)

Bakhtin, M. (1984) *Rabelais and his world.* Helene Iswolsky, Trans. Bloomington, IN: U of Indiana Press. (Original work published 1965.)

Bakhtin, M. (1986). *Speech genres & other late essays.* V. W. McGee, Trans. Austen, TX: U of Texas Press.

Besnier, N., and Street, B. (1994). Aspects of literacy. In T. Ingold (Ed.) *Encyclopedia of anthropology* (pp. 527–562). New York: Taylor & Francis.

Brandt, D., and Clinton, K. (2002). Limits of the local: Expanding perspectives on literacy as a social practice. *Journal of Literacy Research* 34(3), 337–356.

Clifton, J., and Sigoloff, J. (2013). Writing as dialogue across difference: Inventing genres to support deliberative democracy. *English Journal* 103(2), 73–84.

Cushman, E. (2013). *Cherokee syllabary: Writing the people's perseverance.* Norman, OK: U of Oklahoma Press.

Donehower, K., Hogg, C., and Schell, E. (2007). *Rural literacies (Studies in writing and rhetoric).* The Conference on College Composition and Communication.

Edmiston, B. (2013). *Transforming teaching and learning with active and dramatic approaches: Engaging students across the curriculum.* New York: Routledge.

Fecho, B. (2004). *Is this English? Race, language, and culture in the classroom.* New York: Teachers College Press.

Freire, P. (1970). *Pedagogy of the oppressed.* Myra Bergman Ramos, Trans. New York: Continuum Publishing Company.

García, O., and Li Wei. (2014). *Translanguaging: Language, bilingualism, and education.* Basingstoke: Palgrave Macmillan.

Gee, J. P. (1991). *Social linguistics: Ideology in discourses.* London: Falmer Press.

Gee, J. P. (2003). *What video games have to teach us about learning and literacy.* NY: St. Martin's Press.

Gonzalez, L. (2015). Multimodality, translingualism, and rhetorical genre studies. *Composition Forum.* Vol 31. Retrieved from: http://compositionforum.com/issue/31/multimodality.php

Green, B., and Corbett, M. (2013). *Rethinking rural literacies: Transnational perspectives.* NY: Palgrave.

Hacking, I. (2007). Kinds of people: Moving targets. *British Academy Lecture* 11 April 2006.

Hermans, H., and Hermans-Konopka, A. (2010). *Dialogical self theory: Positioning and counter-positioning in a globalizing society*. Cambridge: Cambridge UP.

Higgins, L., Long, E., and Flower, L. (2006). Community literacy: A rhetorical model for personal and public inquiry. *Community Literacy Journal* 1(1), 9–43.

Jocson, K. M. (2008). *Youth poets: Empowering literacies in and out of schools*. New York: Peter Lang.

Kinloch, V. (2009). *Harlem on our minds: Place, race, and the literacies of urban youth*. Columbia, NY: Teachers College Press.

Kirkland, D. (2008). "The Rose that grew from concrete": Postmodern blackness and the new English education. *The English Journal* 97(5), 69–75.

Kirkland, D. (2009). Researching and teaching literacy in the digital dimension. *Research in the Teaching of English* 44(1), 8–22.

Long, E., Jarvis, J., and Deerheart Raymond, D. (2013). The Nipmuck people do exist: Imagining the what next—an experimental alternative to evidentiary legal discourse. In C. Wilkey and N. Mauriello (Eds.) *Texts of consequence: Composing rhetorics of social activism for the writing classroom* (pp. 317–348). Cresskill: Hampton P.

Lu, M.-Z., and Horner B. (2016). Introduction: Translingual work. *College English* 78(3), 207–218.

Mack, K. (2012). *Representing the race: The creation of the civil rights lawyer*. Cambridge: Harvard UP.

Meacham, S., Anderson, M. A., and Correa, C. (2013). Coining phrases for dollars: Jay-Z, economic literacy, and the educational implications of hip hop's entrepreneurial ethics. *International Journal of Critical Pedagogy* 4(3), 69–82.

Morrell, E., and Duncan-Andrade, J. (2002). Promoting academic literacy with urban youth through engaging hip-hop culture. *The English Journal* 91(6), 88–92.

Morrell, E., Dueñas, R., Garcia, V., and Lopez, J. (2013). *Critical media pedagogy: Teaching for achievement in city schools*. New York: Teachers College Press.

Paris, D. (2010). Texting identities: Lessons for classrooms from multiethnic youth space. *English Education* 42(3), 278–292.

Paris, D. (2013). *Language across difference: Ethnicity, communication, and youth identities in changing urban schools*. Cambridge: Cambridge UP.

Powell, M. (2014). A basket is a basket because …: Telling a Native rhetorics story. In J. H. Cox and D. H. Justice (Eds.) *Oxford handbook of indigenous American literature*. New York: Oxford University Press. Retrieved from http://www.oxfordhandbooks.com/view/10.1093/oxfordhb/9780199914036.001.0001/oxfordhb-9780199914036-e-037

Purcell-Gates, V. (2013). Literacy worlds of children of migrant farmworker communities: Participating in a migrant head start program. *Research in the Teaching of English* 48(1), 68–97.

Research at Facebook (2015). The not-so-universal language of laughter. Retrieved from https://research.facebook.com/blog/the-not-so-universal-language-of-laughter/

Rosenblatt, L. (1995). *Literature as exploration* (5th edition). New York: Modern Language Association.

San Pedro, T. (2015). Silence as shields: Agency and resistances among students in the urban southwest. *Research in the Teaching of English* 50(2), 138–153.

Selasie, T. (2015). Taiye Selasie: Don't ask where I'm from, ask where I'm a local. [Video file]. Retrieved from https://www.ted.com/talks/taiye_selasi_don_t_ask_where_i_m_from_ask_where_i_m_a_local?language=en

Smith, F. (2005). *Reading without nonsense* (4th edition). New York: Teachers College Press.

Smith, L. (1999). *Decolonizing methodologies: Research and indigenous peoples.* London: Zed Books.

Sondheim, S. (2011). Finishing the hat. *Look, I made a hat: Collected lyrics (1981–2011) with attendant comments, amplifications, dogmas, harangues, digressions, anecdotes, and miscellany.* New York: Alfred A. Knopf.

Steinkuehler, C. (2008). Cognition and literacy in massively multiplayer online games. In J. Coiro, M. Knobel, C. Lankshear, and D. Leu (Eds.) *Handbook of research on new literacies* (pp. 611–634). New York: Taylor & Francis.

Street, B. (1995). *Social literacies: Critical approaches to literacy in development, ethnography, and education.* Longman: London.

Vološinov, V. N. (1986). *Marxism and the philosophy of language.* L. Matejka and R. Titunik, Trans. Cambridge, MA: Harvard University Press. (Original work published 1929.)

Young, V. A., Barrett, R., Young-Rivera, Y., and Lovejoy, K. B. (2014). *Other people's English: Code-meshing, code-switching, and African-American literacy.* New York: Teachers College P.

4

IDENTITIES, LITERACIES, LEARNING, CULTURES, AND THE DIALOGICAL SELF

Imagine a young man—call him Isaac—sitting in a fast food restaurant talking into an audio recorder. He's a participant in a study that's trying to understand why some working-class young men embrace reading and writing for their own needs outside of school. It's no great educational secret that young men in general are less likely than young women to read or write for their own purposes (Smith & Wilhelm, 2002) and that the dropout event rate for students living in low-income families has, at times, been as much as four times greater than the rate of their peers from high-income families (Laird, DeBell, & Chapman, 2006). Still, against these odds and frequently without support from schools, we've known young men raised in working-class and working-poor communities who have used reading and writing as a means to make sense of the lives they were constructing.

Isaac was one such young man. As he sat talking amid the din of food timers chirping and trays being emptied, Isaac labored to clarify a thought:

> Like, at the point I was at, I was just obsessed with shadow and the fact that I felt like something was always following and pointing its finger at me, you know, mocking me in every way and there was nothing I could do about it. I felt like, at the time, that I should delve deeper into those emotions and see how far they went, kind of the aspect of C. S. Lewis, how far does the rabbit hole go? And I thought by embracing that, instead of not trying to avoid, it would become better, when it really didn't. I started getting more and more depressed and suicidal and [doing] a lot of things that I wish I hadn't done … and like I said, exploded on a lot of people that I didn't really want to. [Pause] It was just the way I was at the time.

Struggling with bipolar disorder and, in this instance, depression, Isaac was laying out the ways he used his literacy skills to make meaning of a self that was "multi-voiced, yet … coherent and open to contradictions" (Hermans & Hermans-Konopka, 2010, p. 5). He read and he wrote with the intent to develop some acceptance of the absurdly random mix of elements that conspired against him even while he tried to construct an identity that would place him less on the margins of the rural southern town where he lived.

This excerpt gives insight into Isaac's struggles and coping mechanisms. In referring to shadow, he suggested the darkness paranoia cast over his life, the relentless way it stalked him. He gets the C. S Lewis reference wrong, or at least mixes allusions—we suspect he meant another Lewis, namely Lewis Carroll of *Alice Through the Looking Glass* fame—yet nevertheless hints at his immersion in literature, especially fantasy literature. By discussing his need to "delve deeper into those emotions"—and the context suggests this delving was done through writing—Isaac revealed his attempt to use literacy to come to terms with the intangible struggles of his life, although admitting that such writing also seemed to feed the problems. The last line, delivered somewhat as a coda to his utterance, is more a shrug of resignation than a full embracing acceptance of his condition.

Isaac was involved in an existential process, as are we all. In *Existentia Africana* Lewis Gordon (2000) has argued that all humans are constructors of meaning, that in trying to make sense of who we are becoming within the contexts with which we transact we are existentialists. Perhaps not existentialists in the grand European tradition of Camus and Sartre, but existentialists because, like those men of letters, we all generate and tether together what meaning we can from our experiences. Furthermore, he asserted that the more a life has been relegated to the margins by random events primarily out of our control—the children of migrant parents, a skin color that doesn't match the dominant culture, a minority religion, a scorned nationality, a too obvious scar or too blatant birthmark—the more those who construct those lives work at making meaning of the cruel randomness of such marginalization. As poet Lucy Grealy (2003) who lost a third of her jaw to cancer attested, "I spent five years of my life being treated for cancer, but since then I've spent fifteen years being treated for nothing other than looking different from everyone else" (back cover).

Interestingly, Camus was born into a poor family in Algeria—two factors of his experience that positioned him somewhat outside the French intelligentsia mainstream. In his semi-autobiographical novel published posthumously (1996), he wrote about what school, learning, and the support of a caring teacher meant for how he came to continually understand the world. When told he was being awarded the Nobel Prize for literature, Camus (1996) stated in a letter of gratitude to his teacher that "my first thought, after my mother, was of you" (p. 319). As you read the novel, which closely parallels Camus's life, you sense that he was thankful, not for an education that merely passed down learning as if it were a torch to uncritically bear, but for an education that illuminated the world around him, allowing him to construct his own understandings. So perhaps, all of us who labor to develop our cohesive and multiple self are more like Camus than we think.

Which brings us back to Isaac, and the ways literacies and how we learn enable or hinder our constructions of meaning and identity. In this chapter, through Isaac and Sam, a female-to-male transgender youth drawing genderless plants, we throw our gaze on identity construction and the role we in education play in helping students use their burgeoning engagement with literacies to live a life examined, a life in process, a life under construction.

Constructing Identities   *Being, doing, becoming*

In thinking about identity construction, we consider identities in terms of iterative and ongoing processes of *being* and *doing* and *becoming*. A person's multiple I-positions are in dialogue emerging, shifting, intersecting, diverging, unfolding, and reconfiguring internally and externally across contexts and over time. A person is always oriented toward the past and the present and the future, with his kinetic potential in the throes of both *being* and *becoming*, and these ways of *being* and *becoming* are often contested and negotiated through ongoing dialogue with the self and with others, sometimes made visible through what a person is *doing*. What a person is *doing* in relation to others also creates a possible touch point for ongoing negotiation of individual as well as shared *being* and *becoming*.

Maintaining these processes is particularly important because of some of the pervasive ways identities are defined and policed as people try to stabilize complexity or mark clear insiders and outsiders or as people talk about what's most important with regard to identity, sometimes framed as uncovering an already-existing essence or "finding oneself", focusing on actions, or orienting toward future possibility. There is something useful about thinking and talking about identity in these ways, but in isolation, there is also something limiting and even potentially harmful. In isolation, any of these ways of thinking and talking about identity only get at part of the story.

Rather than focusing on or prioritizing the truth or falsity of an identity (Is there scientific evidence? Is a person this or that?), we instead ask what kinds of identities—multiple, historical, intersectional, intersubjective—are being *produced* during a given moment and what is at stake in their making. In particular, we highlight the relationship between the ways an identity is constituted and the ways an identity is performed in ever-shifting, mutually constituting situations in which people are acting on and being acted upon by other individuals, groups, texts, and technologies.

Theories of performativity understand the use of signs, symbols, and language to be a form of symbolic action, but not in the cause and effect way we sometimes think of action, in which one act brings about, at some point in the future, a particular effect, nor in the theatrical sense of performance in which an audience watches the drama and spectacle of a performance. Instead, performativity recognizes that signs, symbols, and language are often used to directly address others and in addressing them, they "enact, through their very utterance, the effects they so name" (Happe, 2013, p. 135).

Judith Butler's (1993) well-known example "It's a girl!" comes to mind, in which a person's gendered identity is constituted and the process of "girling" begun in the act of naming before that person has had very little opportunity to do much else but cry (p. 232). These performative utterances have a profound effect on an individual and on the world, on how a person comes to see herself and what she and others think is possible, or not, for her. This initiation into "girling" is based on perceived and *imposed* differences (Salih, 2002, p. 61), and these performative utterances have a profound effect on who a person sees herself *being* or *becoming* and, as that particular kind of person, what options are available to her or not available to her for *doing*. It's important, then, to consider the ways we name and constitute each other and what is enacted in those utterances and what those utterances demand, allow, or limit.

In performative utterances like "It's a girl!" language and symbols are not leveraged as an appeal but as a performance addressed to someone or some group. These performative acts implicitly or explicitly work to define and produce a person's identity, constituting the subjectivity of the person addressed; that is, they enact *subjects* and, in so doing, create an I-position. Take, for example, a marriage ceremony and the performance of "I do," which constitutes a person as a spouse in ways he was not prior to being addressed with those words. In these performances, a subject is constituted in the very act of being addressed, something made possible by previous iterations. The historical nature of these performances teaches people how others see them and cues them about what's expected by others. The historical nature of these performances also bends those involved, both those addressed and those addressing, toward consent to and participation in the social order and social norms these performances invoke.

a subject is constituted

Over time, through recurring social situations and repeated performances, some of these subject positions are normalized and can seem common sense, as if they are not constructed at all but simply "the way things are." As people come to think of the current state of affairs or familiar ways of performing what it means to be a girl or a Native American or a student (or whatever) as "the way things are," and especially as "the way things should be" rather than a historical and discursive and ideological social construction continually being negotiated, they tend to base understanding and instruction and judgments on knowledge claims that assume that particular markers necessarily signify a certain identity. This phenomenon is at work in Sam's experience, described later in this chapter, when others look to external genitalia as the sole, factual marker of gender. When people don't see identity markers as signs, as the historically and socially constructed *signifiers* they are, social constructions are taught and policed as unchangeable facts to which others need to conform.

Performativity shifts our attention from knowledge claims about identity to the discourse around identity construction and to the social, economic, and political materialities those discourses effect. In other words, how do we account for how discourse *produces* identities in ways that can "appear before, or outside of, actual language practices" (Happe, 2013, p. 132), especially as those discourses and identities become normalized over time? What are the effects of discursive practices on our ways of being and doing and becoming? Focusing on the discursive construction of identity leads us to also ask just whose interests do particular identities serve, to what end, and at what cost?

All identities can in some way be challenged and redefined or "looped back" (Hacking, 2007). Of course, there are limits on this. There are some identity markers we cannot change, like our skin color or whether we were born deaf or whether we lose a limb in a car wreck or which side of a national border we're born on. Scott Richard Lyons (2010) calls these "x-marks: contaminated, coerced signs of consent made under conditions not of our making but with hopes of a better future" (p. 40). On their own, these and other x-marks need not signify anything about a person's identity; it is when these signs and symbols are imbued with historical and symbolic meaning recognized by others that they speak to us and to others about our identity, about our place in the world. There is, then, a kind of intertextuality to identity construction: we begin with markers that carry someone else's meanings, that place us in a social location, that tell us what is possible and what is off limits to someone like us. What we do with these markers imbued with historical meanings helps to shape who we are and the cultures we find ourselves part of, and works to reinscribe those limits or transform limits into possibilities.

Of course, this historical connection—what Lyons refers to as "contaminated" and "coerced" symbols and meanings we might not have chosen for ourselves— also means that while we can respond to what came before, we cannot sever the connection. It also means that discussions of authenticity are all but pointless, except to reinscribe definitions and relationships that came before. Missing from discussions of someone's "true" identity is the "recognition that identities are constructed; that they do not come from biology, soil, or the whims of a Great Spirit, but from discourse, action, and history; and finally that this thing is not so much a thing at all, but rather a social process" (Lyons, p. 40), an ongoing artful dialogue. As such, these x-marks aren't an essence—they aren't who you are and who'll you'll only ever be—they are just factors that play into how you continue to construct yourself—at times counting more, at times counting less, but always counting to some extent.

Rather than focusing on the fact of identity, which often shows up in performative utterances that seek to determine and define what is and what counts, instead we would do well to turn our attention to what we are doing with the materials out of which our identities are made—how we are understanding their origins, their logics, and implications; what we recognize as their affordances and constraints; and what else we adapt and invent with others to move toward ideological becoming. The materials and the identities they point to are historically produced: constituted in writing and laws and test scores, on census documents and employment forms and college applications, through social relationships and perceptions of skin or eye color or hair texture or language or clothes, and of course, in the ongoing internal negotiations of a dialogical self. They are sometimes fashioned at a local church service or powwow grounds or pep rallies, sometimes in books or posters or memes. They appear in movies, during halftime, on syrup bottles, on butter packages, on billboards, on T-shirts (Lyons, 2010).

To an extent, identity construction is not unlike constructing understanding from a text. As you read, you ask questions of that text (e.g., Why is this character behaving this way? What was the significance of that event?) in your attempt to make sense of what you are reading. So, too, you ask questions of yourself as you engage the many contexts of your existence.

Perhaps the most important questions you can ask yourself about your identities are these: What will you do with those markers and with those prior meanings and with the aims of others in upholding those meanings? What old markers and meanings will you call on, and how and why? What new markers and meanings will you create, and how and why? What else will these old–new combinations create for you, for others? What logics and values and relationships do these ways of *doing* identity allow or deny you and others?

These questions are important because identities are not fixed or innate or self-evident; they are collective and ongoing constructions of meaning, inseparable from the signs, symbols, and language that give shape and definition to the humanity of an individual body or community of people. Of course, the ways we read what these signs signify can lead to material results, among them rights, responsibilities, privileges, debts, discriminations, stereotypes, citizenships, and the ways you might be treated by the police, the state, teachers, parents, or students. Consider Michel Foucault's observations about previous eras in which a person might steal or engage in non-normative sexual practices, and might even be judged and punished for them, without acquiring a new identity in the process. Now, if someone breaks a law, that person becomes a "criminal"; if someone sleeps with someone of the same sex, that person becomes a "homosexual" (Lyons, 2010, p. 45).

Identities are not only symbolic, dialogic constructions; they are deeply connected to our material, political world. As Linda Martin Alcoff and Satya Mohanty (2006) have written, "identities are not our mysterious inner essences but rather social embodied facts about ourselves in our world; moreover, they are not mere *descriptions* of who we are but, rather, *causal explanations* of our social locations" (p. 6), emphasis in original. Our identities are a kind of a working theory, a simultaneous ongoing synthesis, performance, and testing of possibilities regarding what's good, what's useful, what's valued in us in relation to others. We construct our identities in back and forth dialogical performances through which we negotiate individual and shared meaning at the nexus of personal intentions and social constraints.

What perhaps hasn't been as obvious to this point, but certainly implied throughout the book, is that all of this dialogue across cultures and within the self is not meant for students alone. As teachers, we do not stop our own process of becoming the moment the state approves our certification. There is no credentialing of identity. Instead, like our students, we continue to respond to ever-changing contexts and develop, though perhaps not always realize, more nuanced understandings daily. Teachers' ongoing engagement with their identities through literacy practices is as crucial for them as it is for their students.

Some Reminders and Some New Connections

Earlier in the book we discussed Bakhtin's (1981) argument that response and understanding are irrevocably connected, that it is through response that people create meaning. Response is unavoidable; what someone utters is enmeshed in a web of responses that builds on that which has come before and inclines them toward the responses to come. Likewise, meaning is layered on meaning, both individually and collectively, becoming soaked through with the thoughts of others, yet creating new patterns of ideas as former and current understandings bleed together. What you mean at any given moment is a complicated amalgamation of all you have meant before and all that others have meant before, as well as whatever new understandings you are constructing out of that mix.

Similarly, who you are becoming—that self composed of many I-positions—is saturated with the many experiences that have come your way since minute one. In some ways, you have always been you and in some ways you have never been you; it's just that you are never the same you twice as contexts are ever shifting. Nor do we ever become a new person, rather we are always adding and developing new voices in the mix—voices that mesh and clash in new ways with all of your other voices, contributing to a growing set of possible transactions. Sandra Cisneros (1991) echoes this in her celebrated short story "Eleven":

> What they don't understand about birthdays and what they never tell you is that when you're eleven, you're also ten, and nine, and eight, and seven, and six, and five, and four, and three, and two, and one. And when you wake up on your eleventh birthday you expect to feel eleven, but you don't. You open your eyes and everything's just like yesterday, only it's today. And you don't feel eleven at all. You feel like you're still ten. And you are—underneath the year that makes you eleven.

Similarly, the noted contemporary philosopher Bruce Springsteen remarked once in an interview that we never leave part of our identity behind, that the timid child, the rebellious adolescent, the unfaithful lover, the unfettered rock enthusiast, the chastened son are all in the car as we speed down life's highway. They're all in there with our current self at the wheel listening to the many perspectives and trying to steer some course that makes sense for the future. Some of those voices may have less relevance and impact than they may have once had—for example, the rebellious adolescent rarely gets his way anymore—but he's still taking up a seat and biding his time.

And, just like understanding, we always construct identity in context, and that context seems broader and more dynamic than it has ever been in the past. In a world that enables individuals to have virtual access to even remote corners of the planet and where multinational corporations blur economic and political boundaries, globalization encounters what Hermans and Hermans-Konopka (2010) deemed to be a "counterforce"—localization. The cultures of our neighborhoods, our cities, and our nation states are repeatedly and more routinely subjected to transactions with neighborhoods, cities, and nation states that heretofore had only occasional or less contact. The impact of this burgeoning dialogue is not lost on the individual. The centrifugal and centripetal relationship between globalization and localization is "reflected in the mini-society of the self" and can result in either "identity confusion" or a "higher level of integration" (p. 3).

Therefore, people exist in a dialogical mesh in which our many I-positions and many contexts continuously transact—you are the other and the other is you. Such a high degree of flux often manifests in a high degree of uncertainty that, depending somewhat on perspective and response, can be seen as "a gift … [that] opens a broad range of unexpected possibilities" or an anxiety and insecurity-laden morass (Hermans & Hermans-Konopka, 2010, p. 3). Coping with and even embracing this uncertainty through dialogical response leads to a realization that more than "just a positive or negative feeling state," uncertainty is an expected "experiential feature of a self in action" (p. 5). Uncertainty, no matter how it might cause our belief system to wobble, is necessary for our ongoing construction of understanding and identity.

Take, for example, Scott Richard Lyons' (2010) 12-year-old daughter and her girlfriends, all dressed in colorful regalia, walking around conspicuously in front of a group of boys on the last night of a powwow. A boy, not dressed for dancing, called Lyons' daughter a "White girl," intending to insult her for being fair-skinned and light-haired like her blonde Norwegian mother. Lyons surmises that perhaps the boy was engaging in some weird preteen form of flirting, but his daughter was not particularly impressed. Instead, she replied powerfully in sharp *Ojibwemowin:* "Gaawin, nid Anishinaakbekwe! Ogiimaabinesiik indizhinikaaz, awaazisii indoodem, Gaa-zagaskwaajimekaag nindonjibaa! Ginisidotam ina?" After telling the boy that she was, in fact, an Ojibwe girl with a name, a clan, and a nation, she asked if he understood, but it was clear that he did not. "Then why don't you speak for yourself!" shouted a darker-skinned girlfriend, leaving the boy looking sheepish and perhaps feeling a little less Ojibwe. In this case of policing identity, Lyons' daughter "used language to trump phenotype, wielding one authenticity over another" (p. 35).

That night Lyons' daughter "spoke for herself and redefined that thing we call Native identity in the very heart of Indian space." However, two years later Lyons overheard her referring to herself as a "White girl." Two years after that, he explains that she started calling herself "multiracial." Lyons reflects: "I have always told her that she is Ojibwe, and an Ojibwe person is a complicated thing to be" (p. 36). And we would add that all people, no matter how they self-identify or what I-position seems to be most prominent, are complicated things to be.

However, human existence is often more complicated for some—unjustly and randomly so—than it is for others. If you primarily exist in a context where your race, your gender, your sexual preference, your socioeconomic class, your religion, your physical capacity, the words you choose, the pronunciations you utter, the clothes you wear, the thoughts you manifest, and/or the positions you take basically constitute the cultural codes of power, you have little motivation to call any of that into question. Where is the wobble bringing those constructions into uncertainty? On the other hand, those cultural groups more marginalized from the center—for example, working-class African Americans negotiating systemic racism in the United States, Palestinians living within the contested borders of Israel, the Kurdish minority in Iraq trusting neither ISIS nor the government in Baghdad, gays and lesbians in the US reading mixed messages from the heteronormic majority—have a deep need to respond to the uncertainty manifested in the heightened complexity of their political and social contexts. It is in response to such uncertainty that Franz Fanon, as discussed by Lewis Gordon (2000), called for a pedagogy to build a questioning humanity.

But the goal cannot be to bring people from the margins to the center but instead to "destabilize" the hegemonic core (Dhaliwal, 1996, p. 44), inviting ongoing dialogue. In an essay, the title of which merits mentioning—"Choosing the Margin as a Space of Radical Openness"—bell hooks (1990) argued that those who the dominant powers have *relegated* to the margins need to, instead, *choose* to position themselves there, to see it as a radicalizing space. It is there, in a "site of creativity and power" (p. 152) as well as resistance, that the oppressed can look toward the center, see it differently, call it into question, challenge its constructions, and offer other voices, other ways of knowing. To radicalize the margins is not only to envision and construct possibilities for thriving on the fringes but also to rewrite the metaphor of "center"—to *de-center* while also inventing lively and powerful alternative "centers." Such positioning involves struggle, but from novelist Alice Walker we know there is "joy in the struggle" (cited in Fecho, 2011, p. 110) and, again from hooks, "struggle to be that which pleasures, delights, and fulfills desire" (p. 153).

From this theoretical dialogue, we intuit a number of assumptions about the role of meaning making in our lives, particularly as it relates to identity construction. To start, all learners carry the responsibility of making meaning for themselves as well as making meaning for the greater cultures at large. We are individuals within social structures and therefore have responsibility both to ourselves and to those structures. Literary scholar Terry Eagleton (2007) has used the analogy of a jazz ensemble as an example for humanity to follow. As he noted, a jazz group's complex harmony "comes not from playing from a collective score, but from the free musical expression of each member acting as the basis for the free expression of others" (pp. 171–173). There is a cohesive and elegant whole that comes out of this musical dialogue, but not at the sacrifice of the musical utterances of individual musicians. Rather it is their individual expressions authored in response to each other that moves the piece coherently forward; the individual contributes to and gains from the collective without being completely subsumed by the group.

A second idea is that meaning is made and identity constructed through language; without the abilities to express ourselves in a variety of ways, humans would be unable to generate meaning within their contexts. We are operating with a broad view of language; for us, the musical expression of that jazz band is language, as are the codes read by computers, the images produced through many kinds of art, and the movements and poses performed as dance. As Maxine Greene (2001) rhapsodized, "Young and old flower when given opportunities to inscribe images, to express their feelings in *some significant language*" (p. 96, we've added the italics). The implication of *some significant language* encompasses dance, music, craft, painting, sculpture, and the full range of artistic, scientific, and, indeed, human expression.

Psychological researchers Travis Proulx and Steven Heine (2009) have demonstrated that, when confronted by thoughts or events that seem to make no sense, our minds seek out patterns. In one of their studies, participants who first read a nonlinear, absurdist, Kafkaesque short story were better able to discern patterns in seemingly random strings of letters than were those who had read a more linear and tidy version of the story. Proulx and Heine surmised that when faced with complexity and unclear meaning, participants sought meaning in everything around them more aggressively. Writing in the *The New York Times*, Maria Konnikova (2015) echoed the conclusions of this study when she offered that "human nature is wired toward creating meaning out of meaninglessness" and that "nobody wants reality to resemble a Kafka novel." One way that people stave off a Kafkaesque reality is to actively construct through language, in all its many forms, who they are continually becoming.

Third, as language remains in process and subject to centripetal and centrifugal forces, so do our attempts to make meaning. On one hand, dominant cultural forces exist that try to reify meaning—to have us all believe and perhaps act as one. Our multiple I-positions are often pressed by society to conform to certain expectations: Why did you not grieve when your mother died?; If he's running for President, he needs to be a Christian; A real man wouldn't take that from a woman; Oh she's an Oreo, an apple, a coconut; Why didn't you stand for the playing of the national anthem? Lyons (2012, July 16), a confident scholar of Native American studies, is not immune to the reaches of such pressure:

> Apparently I'm not a real Indian. Apparently, going to grad school and questioning how Native people are portrayed in pop culture makes me less "real." I knew, in starting this blog, that being a white-looking Cherokee from SoCal trying to talk about Native issues would cause some problems.
>
> *(Paragraph 1)*

All about us, in ways overt and tacit, blatant and subtle, from seemingly innocuous through to viciously malignant, the cultures in which we participate possess and operationalize expectations of conformity.

Still, continually and often with vigor, we as individuals push back on these expectations. Despite the enormity of the tug toward unification, a range of less dominant cultural and even individual forces exist that resist this reification by raising questions, offering critique, supporting alternate considerations, and the like. In doing so, people blur the lines at the boundary of these cultural positions. Someone can be Black and a conservative on political issues, Catholic and a supporter of LGBTQ rights, a feminist and concerned about unfettered abortions or in favor of pornography. As individuals we constantly chip away at dogma, at policy, at convention. For a small, but vital example, visit any school where students are required to wear uniforms and you'll still see discreet but significant expressions of individuality: a small, but visible tattoo, loud socks peeking out from under khakis; asymmetrical haircuts; a brash assortment of rings and bracelets. Conformity to a point; individuality to a point.

However, the day-to-day chipping away that a person does is neither mere deconstruction of conformity nor mere discovery of a pre-existing self. There is a seemingly apocryphal story—attributed to a range of sculptors and art critics— that sculpting merely requires chipping away all that is extraneous. What remains is the essence of what you sought to create. Therefore, if sculpting an elephant, chip away all the marble that isn't elephant. Many people see identity this way, as a search. People of this mindset seek identity, view the process as a diving inward and a whacking away all bits that aren't who they are, that eventually they will *uncover* and *find* who they are. We posit here, somewhat paraphrasing Yoda, there is no *is*, nor do people participate in acts of identity attrition. Instead, there's only *being and doing and becoming* and an ongoing construction through an accumulation of transactional and dialogical experiences,

being, doing, becoming

Learning through Isaac and Sam

If you were fortunate enough to see the movie *Steve Jobs* starring Michael Fassbender, you were able to witness a prime example of someone negotiating multiple positions within the self. For those who missed the movie—how did you let it go by?—the writer, Aaron Sorkin, set the movie on the days of three key product launches in Jobs' early career—the original Macintosh, the ill-fated NEXT, and the iMac. On all three days spread across a dozen or so years, he has encounters with his chief assistant, his original innovation partner; his business mentor and father figure; his ex-girlfriend, the daughter he at first denies, and his chief programmer. Over the course of the movie, Jobs shifts through at least these I-positions if not more: boss, CEO, entrepreneur, ex-lover, father, friend, innovator, media icon, orphan, partner, surrogate son. Very often one or more of these positions are at odds with the others. In one scene, Jobs the boss is trying to nail down all the details of the launch while Jobs the ex-lover and Jobs the father are being confronted about increasing child support, Jobs the burgeoning tech icon is polishing his public image, Jobs the friend is taking a stand opposite that of his innovation partner, and Jobs the orphan and surrogate son are seeking support from his mentor.

You can imagine the complexity of dialogue shifting across these somewhat dovetailing, somewhat conflicting positions. Of course, although the movie is about an actual person and based on a biography of him, it remains a fictionalized and dramatized account of events in his life. Certainly some aspect of all these complex transactions occurred around these key events in the life of Steve Jobs, but the screenwriter used juxtaposition to bring them to the forefront. Yet, we argue, the scene above only differs from what most of us go through daily only in this dramatic juxtaposition and the compression of time. If anything, your day-to-day dialogical transactions are even more complex and, through the remainder of this section, we focus on how that complexity transacts with adolescents trying to make sense of such complexity. We reintroduce you to Isaac and introduce you to Sam as we show the ways they used literacy practices to generate ongoing and meaning-making dialogues within themselves and with the various cultural contexts of their lives. In doing so, they engaged in what Bakhtin (1981) and Freire (1970) have called a *process of becoming*.

Isaac

A prolific reader and writer—he started doing both at length as soon as he entered school, according to his parents—Isaac was a reflective, articulate, and questioning adolescent. Curiously, his being diagnosed as bipolar created a focus in his life around which many of his attempts to garner meaning were gathered. Not having intended to be bipolar—who has?—Isaac instead had to daily come to grips with this x-mark, one whose circumstances filled his life with uncertainties. Growing up in farm country just outside the reach of the northeast suburbs of Atlanta at the time of Bob's work with him, he was a senior in his high school. Due to many absences, disciplinary actions, and his placement for a time in an alternative high school—all events that were in some way connected to his bipolarity—Isaac was three credits shy of the minimum requirement and thus was unable to graduate with his class that spring. Instead he had to finish one more elective in the ensuing autumn.

Although he used reading, writing, and artistic rendering to respond to the uncertainties the bipolarity visited upon him, our focus—purely due to limited space—is on how Isaac used writing to dialogue with his various I-positions and the various contexts those I-positions inhabited. As he matured, Isaac's immersion in literacy practices was a deliberate attempt on his part to use these mediums for dialogue. As he noted:

> I believe, at the same time, a lot of [my trying to cope with my condition] is what has compelled me to read and write. A lot of that is what fueled it because [of] that constant contemplation, that all the time I'm trying to

better myself. Although [my searching for answers] may have been destructive for the most part, it also made me pretty much who I am to this point and I've been trying to cope with the fact that I'll be losing that.

The theme of "bettering" himself flows throughout the recorded interviews with Isaac, as does his conflict with seeing his attempts to make meaning as often being destructive. His responses to his bipolarity frequently led him to inner dialogue with I-positions to which he was simultaneously tugged toward and repelled by. The offhand comment "I'll be losing that" refers to a worry that the uncertainty of living with his condition might result in the loss of some essential part of the self he had constructed to date. Even as he sought to develop other ways of presenting himself to the world, he, like many people, clung to the idea that there was an essence that could be lost and found.

It may be no surprise that a young man with sensitivity and introverted tendencies would be drawn to poetry, perhaps partly as a creative outlet, but mainly as a way to make meaning of his complex existence. Isaac's continued ambivalence about his bipolarity was rendered in the excerpt below, which ends a poem he had written in his ongoing attempts to better understand the multiple ways he dialogued with the shifting contexts he encountered daily. In it—rendered exactly as he wrote it—Isaac simultaneously rails against the wind and savors the breeze, curses the dark and lays himself gently in its folds.

> this verse my narcotic
> most better than
> "Cures"
> pills for your "Sanity"
> a "Loss of mental Balance,"
> i might be "insane"
> i might be the ocean
> pushed,
> pulled,
> by tides within'
> I have no control?
> i laugh at the whores
> of this mediocre appoclypse
> wheres god?
> he chose to abbandon,
> when we gave all,
> for thumbs on our hands,
> silly mammal,
> ego hurt?
> the fall from Eden,
> Hell on Earth,

Its a problem
Of tempermeant
Of whoose im unsure,
there's one thing thats certain,
go read a book.

Our intent was not to bring a psychoanalytic stance to this writing. Nor did we take the role of teacher of rhetoric or formal grammarian. Readings of the poem from those perspectives might yield different interpretations. Instead, we chose to view the poem as literacy educators trying to understand a student who is struggling with a complex set of circumstances. In doing so, we see Isaac as a meaning maker, someone who has embraced literacy practice to remain in dialogue with himself and his surroundings.

What stands out to us in this poetic excerpt is how Isaac conveys what it feels like to be caught in the centripetal tug and centrifugal pull of conflicting ways of being in the world, like an ocean jostled "by tides within." Earlier in the excerpt he played with the idea of poetry being a narcotic, one that exceeds other "cures" he has attempted or experienced. The line is almost meta-cognitive in nature, alluding to the process even as he engages in the process. And certainly, a line like "Go read a book" can have many interpretations and implications, however we sense that at least one of the interpretations would call out not only the second positive reference to literacy practice, but also the assuredness with which the line concludes the poem.

Not surprisingly, given his diagnosis, Isaac's writings tended toward themes many might construe as ominous and even nihilistic:

I guess I've always kind of been dark about things, usually during points of depression. It comes from lots of stress or whatever. I just like to basically express myself to that, try to put a little bit of me in everything I do.

Like the poem excerpted above, this response from Isaac indicates an ongoing oppositional pull occurring within him as he regarded his bipolarity. On one hand, somewhat centrifugally, he admitted to a sense that the disease caused him to write in ways and genres that for him were comforting but could be construed as disturbing to others. Conversely, he freely acceded to the idea that these thoughts were ultimately a part of the identity he was constructing, that although his bipolarity didn't completely define him, it was a part of the multiple and cohesive whole which he struggled to understand.

For Isaac, writing was a way of knowing and a deeply personal activity. Most of the writing Isaac attempted when he was in a depressive or manic state he never shared, although he was willing to discuss the process:

Well, they were more like train of thought writings. What it was like, just how the emotion felt, and how I could describe it as best I could through a word and give it a materialistic view. So there were a lot of things that dealt with (pause) turning myself to the shadows, picking my pieces from the sand and try to assemble who or what I might have been. That's about how [the writings] were (pause) just very (pause) depressed, but at the same time, a cloud to where you couldn't really tell what the meaning was unless I could tell you.

The language of this excerpt is particularly telling. Isaac spoke of picking up pieces of who he was and trying to reassemble the whole, not unlike an artisan assembling a mosaic. We argue that such assembling, given the flux of dialogical contexts, never results in a "who or what I might have been," but instead renders a momentary assemblage that positions toward the next delving responses. Regardless, Isaac wrote with the intent to make meaning, even if that meaning might be clouded to others and only discernible by him.

As a writing strategy, Isaac would let words and thoughts flow onto paper. In terms of making sense,

Lots of [the writings] do, some of them don't. Some of them were just hateful, at myself and other people. Those I keep just as a reminder that I could go that far—I'm still human—that type of thing. I really wished I had thought better of myself at the time because I felt like I could have done more now than what I had (pause) but I just let it all go. But if I hadn't done [the actions and thoughts produced by my disorder] at the same time, I wouldn't have been able to make those [mania- and depression-induced writings], and actually see how far I could push myself to any artistic thing.

The complexity of Isaac's attempts to make meaning of his circumstances is readily apparent in this excerpt. He simultaneously rued writing in ways that seemed hurtful to him and others but also realized how exciting it was to be that artistically aware. He understood that his bipolarity made it difficult for him in social circumstances, but also that the heightened awareness could be its own reward. This understanding is similar to ways that Hermans and Hermans-Konopka (2010) used Bakhtin's (1981) ideas on heteroglossia to suggest that identities are always in process, representing ongoing transactions between a unifying identity and various centrifugal identities, which they describe in terms of I-positions. We are simultaneously all those I-positions, with each, to varying degrees, contributing to the whole.

And Isaac seemed to have in perspective the limits of how effective writing could be in terms of changing his world. As he explained,

It helped me through education with my personal experience, but it really didn't help me through the external because [when I went to the alternative high school] and came back, all my friends disappeared.

Isaac realized that the writing could help him come to some understanding of why his friends may have drifted away but, in the end, it wouldn't necessarily bring them back to him. He seemed well aware of the difference between meaning making and problem solving, and that the former didn't necessarily lead to the latter.

Yet Isaac was not without agency, and it was through his embrace of literacy and artistic expression that he found means for making sense, for seeking to use writing as a means for generating possibility.

> I'm trying to express myself now [but] I have a problem [with being open], but I try not to acknowledge it because it's an unnecessary fear and it's something I have to let go of. I want to try to just keep myself in that whole perspective because I don't think there should be any reason to hide anything if you feel honest and open about it. So I figure if I can get myself in that mindset, it may change some things for me.

It was the nature of Isaac's bipolarity to cause him to turn inward, to not share himself, his thoughts, and his emotions with the world around him. It was an effort for him to do otherwise. Yet, as this excerpt indicates, it was an effort he wanted to and did undertake.

When the wobble in our lives becomes too great to be withstood, it needs to be understood. With that intent, we seek dialogue with respected others, knowledgeable texts, and our many identities. Western adolescence being a time of upheaval and shifting perspective, the adolescent's need to make meaning intensifies. As such, educators ought to create room within their practices for this necessary and valuable dialogue. They need to design and implement literacy practice that allows students access to their inner dialogues and means for calling such dialogues forth. As Barbara Kamler (2001) suggested, we who work closely with students need to find ways to help them locate the personal in the academic.

Isaac understood this need. Even more, he understood that dialogue alone will not heal all wounds, although we are convinced that it will make the intolerable more tolerable. Sadly, a short while after high school graduation, Isaac succumbed to an overdose of drugs. We purposely selected *succumbed* over *died* because the former implies a yielding to forces greater than ourselves. We believe Isaac at some point succumbed, but he did not do so without having constructed some understandings for himself and leaving some insights for others. We hope that all students could be afforded the same opportunities.

Sam

"I first realized something wasn't right when I was 6 or 7. I wasn't comfortable in skirts and dresses, or anything else from the girl's department," recalled Sam, today a confident teenager with wavy hair and a trimmed beard. Sam was addressed at birth with the pronouncement, "It's a girl!" but a few years later self-identified as a boy. "I was at a wedding, and I was one of the flower girls, and I had to wear a dress. I was kicking and screaming," remembered Sam. "I took it off and never wore it again. I was at another wedding, and I insisted on wearing a cowboy hat and chaps."

For Sam, these were not merely the inclinations of a young tomboy. Sam resisted not only the social trappings of girlhood; he also resisted being constituted as a girl. Like the 32 transgender children in a study gauging automatic gender associations (Olson, Eaton, & Key, 2015), Sam experienced himself as a boy as much as any cisgender boy might. He asked his family to call him "Sam" rather than the name his parents had initially given him. Even so, Sam remembers that his grandmother "would buy me girls' clothes, and it just wasn't right. And yet every year she'd send a package."

Sam experienced a social contradiction around identity construction that many transgender youth experience. Traditional theories of gender identity recognize that by the age of 6, children have a sense of their own gender, based on the sex assigned at birth, early awareness of that sex assignment, and gender socialization. And yet, if a child deviates from the sex assigned to them at birth or rejects the rules of gender embedded in the socialization process, they are assumed to be too young to know their gender, suffering from either gender confusion or a gender disorder. Following this logic, if you are cisgender, you can know your gender, but if you are transgender or gender non-conforming, you cannot possibly know. Sam, and others like him, then get caught in a space where they do not *do* gender in the ways others think they should, but neither are they granted equal knowledge of gender that other young people are. The only option that is more broadly socially acceptable is one that conforms. However, when identities become about knowledge claims rather than about what people are *being* and *doing* and *becoming* in relation to each other, then identities can become sites of confrontation over power, power regulated by numbers or social hierarchies or social norms.

In elementary school and junior high, Sam primarily saw himself in terms of a gendered self, a boy that others would not see as a boy. Despite his deeply felt sense of self, the message he was getting from many of the people around him was that he was *doing* gender wrong and that *being* a gendered self is fixed and determined by medical professionals delivering a baby. Recent clinical observations and research studies (Steensma et al., 2013) show that, for transgender youth, chromosomes and external genitalia are not the driving forces for these children's identities. Instead, hormones and chemicals in the brain have been found to more directly correlate with gender (Tannehill, 2014), which can, because of the ways genders are assigned to bodies, create a body–brain mismatch.

It becomes clear, though, in talking with Sam now as a high school senior, that this sense of a gendered self trumped other ways he might have seen himself. He later comes to see himself as having multiple I-positions and recounts purposeful ways he navigates and constructs them with others. However, early on his gendered self overshadowed other I-positions he might have otherwise experienced as primary because of the frustration and conflict he experienced when others refused to see him the way he saw himself, when they refused to listen to his experiences and take them seriously.

By junior high, Sam was interested in a girl at his school. When the young lady Sam liked told Sam they couldn't date because they were both girls, Sam replied: "I'll get a sex change. Then we can go out." But she did not see this as a solution and began to bully Sam. "I was in the locker room—the girls' locker room—and she would laugh at me, make fun of me. I wasn't shaving my armpits, and she would say: 'That kid has bad hygiene.' That teasing made me start shaving so that I would present as the person that everyone else wanted me to be." Conforming to others' expectations when they did not match his own internal sense of himself sent Sam into a spiral. Sam's mother remembers, "I had lost my happy kid. Sam was crying all the time. And I was worried. At the time, I was reading research, and the attempted suicide rate amongst trans kids was something like 80 percent. I could force Sam into the gender he was born into. And he might end up in a coffin."

As deeply held as his sense of his own gender was, Sam needed solidarity, needed others to recognize and value him as a boy. Sam and his family turned to a local trans community for help and connection. However, with a body going through puberty and without hormone blockers, the mismatch between Sam's body and his brain chemistry only widened. Thinking back about his experiences, he explains:

> I always felt that everyone in the trans community was so privileged. Everybody, all that I knew, everybody that I knew that was trans was on hormones, they were transitioning, they had their name changed, they were viewed how they wanted to be and it just brought a lot of hatred toward myself because I wasn't there yet because I was so young … I was just sad. I was depressed all the time, and we didn't know what was going on.

Sam felt caught in between worlds, fitting nowhere. This liminal state was one of confusion and frustration and isolation for Sam.

As Sam transitioned into high school, he turned to art and to nonfiction by trans authors to dialogue with the I-position he experienced as most prominent and most oppressed. During his sophomore year, Sam attended the Philadelphia Trans Health Conference, where he was introduced to *Manning up: Transsexual men on finding brotherhood, family, and themselves*, an anthology that offers the stories of 27 men who transitioned from female to male and who write about their experiences of racism, of family, of male privilege, of embodied maleness, of "passing," and of disclosure. Sam describes the book as "a bunch of testimonies by other trans men about finding a sense of self and who they are and after reading that book, it kind of brought light to what everybody else has gone through and I can take control of my life and find my sense of self." Sam recalls being amazed by these men's stories and feeling relieved, thinking for the first time, "I'm trans!" These stories offered Sam a sense of solidarity and comfort he hadn't been able to find elsewhere. He could see, for the first time, a future for himself—one in which he wasn't stuck in between worlds, one in which he could be fully himself. Like Isaac, he also calls on the familiar language of essence, of "finding" himself even though he later talks about his self as dynamic and multifaceted and is attentive to the ways he constructs and projects his multiple I-positions and how they intersect.

Around this same time, Sam began to see an endocrinologist and take hormones so that his body would begin to match his brain chemistry. He also legally changed his name to Sam. As his gendered identity felt more synthesized, he experienced what he calls a sense of peace. In his artwork, he began to imagine alternative ways of thinking about gender. The genderless plants, shown below, are his version of asking, "What if …? What if we didn't mark gender in the ways we do? How would we see one another? How would we relate?" He created these three pieces and several others for an art show about gender with the Trans Spectrum of Arizona (TSAZ) group. He recalls:

> I made a couple plant heads, and then I thought into it more and then I thought that plants don't have an actual visual gender as much as humans do, so I wanted to do something that was related to gender and address it but at the same time totally laugh it into pieces. So I made a ton of plant heads that had very androgynous looking bodies but the plants were how they expressed themselves; they didn't have an actual visual gender so it was just something that lacked it, and I thought that was really cool. Because everybody looks at gender, for like everything. You see someone and the first thing you think is, "What are their pronouns? What are they a male or female?" And that's usually what people think when they first meet someone, and that's when you look at a plant head, you think, "I can't even tell, I just see a plant."

Interestingly, even as some strangers would now see Sam as male, Sam seems to indicate through his plant heads that he would do away with gender as a primary marker of identity. Gender at times takes on a hyper-significance for him in large part because of his social and political struggle with others for recognition and for value. It's this struggle that now informs so much of who Sam is becoming and how he performs his other I-positions as artist or activist.

Sam listed his name on the back of the genderless plant cards and underneath his name he'd written "Trans Artist." When asked about this choice, this intersection, he explained:

> I wanted to make myself more known … as the person who I am, as trans, so … people out there at the school … know there are trans people out there who are there to accept them and help them and, so I wanted to be recognized as more than just an artist or just an activist, but Trans-Artist and Trans-Activist, so people know that there are people out there who are like them, or people who just need representation, and … I wanted to be more known for people who need it.

Even so, 20 minutes later, Sam remarked that this year he has come to see himself as an artist—rather than primarily transgender—because of a different kind of artistic work: "I've found myself in [doing] ceramics." Sam then marked a distinction in the ways he now thinks of himself:

> Well, first and foremost, I definitely think of myself as an artist. Um, that's like, my title, I guess I could say. And then I see myself as trans, for the sake of the community and other younger trans people who need that help. And I definitely view myself as trans only because there are other people who, um, need that visibility, and at a time when we come together or have to stand up as a community, but um, in my own mind I only view myself as male. Because I don't want ... because there's a fear that comes

along with being trans, being different, and I feel that I've always been male, that's who I am. Yeah, trans is a part of my history and it's important, but male is who I am.

For Sam, as his appearance has been less immediately politicized by extended family and strangers, as he has experienced less oppression as trans and has become more accepted as male, and as he has found worthwhile work for himself in making ceramics, he has been able to turn his attention to other interests and projects, and only recently has he come to frame his identity primarily in terms of the work he most wants to do.

The ceramics Sam creates, like the one pictured on p. 113, are often pieces of pottery that do not attempt a message or political provocation like his "plant

heads" do. Instead, as an artist, Sam attends to other conceptual aesthetics and technical aspects of producing art. It is worth noting that there are several times that Sam names as particularly important for his own sense of self: early on when he recognizes himself as male; as a sophomore when he thinks, "I'm trans!" and experiences relief in belonging; in contexts where others might need him to be visible as trans-artist or trans-activist; and when he's doing the work of creating ceramics—work he experiences as rewarding, generative, and difficult, yet within his grasp. These moments sometimes happen all at once, in a flash, but more often, these occurrences unfold slowly over time, leaving plenty of room for thoughtful dialogue with others.

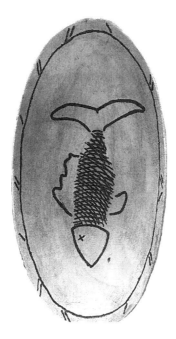

IDENTITY CONSTRUCTION

Framing the Dialogue (Jen)

Bob's sense of texts primarily being windows to see into other's lives or mirrors to reflect our own lives and Jen's sense of texts primarily being important for the ways they support us doing things gives you an idea of the different ways we each think about identity construction. Here, we take up those differences.

Jen's Take

As someone who studies the purposeful ways people leverage language and texts in relation to others and as a pragmatist, I am always interested in the work at hand, the work people see themselves up to with others. Sometimes constructing an identity—as a project in itself—is the primary work at hand. Pascale sees her self, her work that way. Sometimes the project of constructing an identity can hinder and impede other possible work with others. In fact, the synthesizing work of identity construction is also about marking boundaries with others and determining what will not be synthesized. The construction of identity is, in some cases, mostly about marking difference and disrupting and upending others' shared norms.

However, the work of policing identity markers and/or disrupting identity markers can distract from other possible ways of being and doing and becoming together across difference. For example, if the conversation is always about who is Ojibanwe enough—who is in or out—then the conversation is likely *not* about what those who see themselves as Ojibanwe will do together going forward, and it is also likely *not* about the ways other people and other systems would mark all Ojibanwe as outsiders. The young man who polices the ways another Ojibanwe looks misses out on his chance to do anything meaningful with an Ojibanwe girl, let alone what she might have to offer by way of language and cultural practices. Writing with Bob, I found myself trying to mark the importance—or at least the possibility—of identity construction as something that occurs through doing other things with people rather than something to do as a thing in itself.

Bob's Take

For me, identity construction is closely tied to dialogical self theory (Hermans & Hermans-Konopka, 2010), which we've referenced quite often in the main text. In particular, I'm drawn to the idea that I am in the other and the other is in me. We simultaneously shape ourselves while others are also shaping who we are. And it shouldn't be forgotten that we are also shaping others as we shape ourselves. Some of us may go about some aspects of this construction more consciously—and at different times of our lives, some cultural aspects of that construction may take precedence over others—but regardless of where the focus might be, many of our I-positions are under construction simultaneously, and sometimes without full cognizance on our part.

Where I think this dialogue flows for me is in a deep and eddying belief that identities are not fixed nor singular nor based exclusively in some collection of chemicals given to us at birth. Instead, people are enmeshed in constant identity construction, that they are perpetually being, doing, and becoming. Yet in all of that dynamism, they retain traces of all the I-positions they've performed—not as dead relics of the past—but as participants in the ongoing construction. And perhaps to put an exclamation point on what I've just written, I see much of what Jen believes about identity being folded into my enlarging understanding of such constructions.

What We Make of All This

We who teach—art, music, world languages, history, economics, technology, physical education, health, the vocational spectrum, but especially English and language arts—are intimately engaged with students in episodes of and opportunities for identity construction. These transactions occur whether we or they are cognizant of them or not. The trick, then, is to be cognizant, to seize the opportunity and embrace the responsibility. Given the amount of time that students spend physically in school and involved in school-related activities like sports, clubs, and homework, the potential for shaping the process of becoming that all adolescents are faced with is staggeringly large. As students and teachers engage the many rich texts of their lives—print-based, electronic, music, art, video, live encounters—they are also involving the self in multiple internal and external dialogues, all of which contribute to their being and doing and becoming.

There is a somewhat finite group of scholars for whom literature study is a career, and the esoteric and nuanced delving into the complexity of the art form is a primary motivator for reading. Then there's the rest of us. We read because engagements with texts help us to simultaneously make sense of the other and the self. We are doing what Judith Lysaker (2006) calls creating a relationship with text. It's not about *finding* the secrets locked inside *All the Light We Cannot See* or *Bastard Out of Carolina*, it's about interpreting the worlds created and lives lived within those texts and then holding those interpretations up as a mirror and a window related to our own worlds and lived lives. Like spiders, we spin filaments of connections across these texts and our experiences creating a complex web of sturdy, yet tentative understandings—really theories needing further testing—as we continue to read, compose, listen, and talk our way through this ongoing construction.

We also read to *do things* in the world and in the *doing* take up possible ways of *being* and *becoming*. In school, reading and learning are often reduced to decontextualized comprehension in which facts are gleaned, formulas and acronyms memorized, and skills performed and repeated on written tests. Yet, decades' worth of scholarship in literacy studies has shown that a student's ability to remember facts or formulas for a test does not necessarily mean that that student would be able to discern in another situation what to *do* with those facts, or even which facts might be helpful for understanding a phenomenon or for addressing a particular problem in a meaningful way (Barton & Hamilton, 1998; Collins & Blot, 2003; Scribner & Cole, 1981; Gee, 2003).

To isolate knowing from doing is to limit the ways young people imagine possibilities for being and becoming. None of the subjects we teach in schools are merely a collection of static facts. Each is, instead, its own buzzing ecology of activity systems, or as James Gee (2005) puts it, "a 'game' certain types of people 'play'" (p. 34). Using biology as an example, Gee writes:

> These people engage in characteristic sorts of activities, use characteristic sorts of tools and language, and hold certain values; that is, they play by a certain set of "rules". They *do* biology. Of course, they learn, use, and retain lots and lots of facts—even produce them—but the facts come from and with the doing. Left out of the context of biology as activity, biological facts are trivia.

What is the "game" of a language & literacies?

In schools, then, when students are learning biology or art or history, they should be learning to play that "game," to *be* players in that game. For those of us who teach language and literacies, this raises an important question: What is the "game" of language and literacies? What are language and literacies good for in the world? What role might language and literacies play in our everyday lives, in carving out good work with others, in inviting others to share our concerns, in testing out possible futures? For Isaac and Sam—and for Raymond whose work we describe below—*doing* opened up possibilities for new ways of being. Their identity construction was not tied to learning to read and write and design in a "one size fits all" way, but rather to learning to read *as,* to write *as,* to design *as* particular kinds of people engaged in particular kinds of work.

People who *do* biology or photography or ceramics must learn *what* to do and *how* to do. They can't simply make things up as they go; they have to discover what the rules of that "game" are and how they can best be leveraged to accomplish goals. Texts aid in this effort and cue readers about the kinds of things biologists or photographers or ceramics artisans care about and talk about. That is, texts cue readers about kinds of *being* and *doing* to take up, and not take up. It is these two things—the ways we imagine each other and the ways we imagine the work we're doing—that perhaps hold the most serious implications for those of us who teach language and literacies.

Of any writing assessment, Kathleen Yancey (1999) argued that we should ask, "Which self does [this] writing assessment permit … which self does [this] assessment construct?" (p. 484). We might ask this not only about writing assessments, but about all of the texts and activities we encounter and include in our classes. The texts a person reads and writes, the activities a person engages, the recognizable social situations a person finds himself navigating are loaded with material, cognitive, and social implications. They teach a person more than forms, conventions, or methods; they teach a person what is possible—what a person can do and what a person must do in particular situations. They teach, then, what kinds of selves are possible and necessary, and in so doing, routinize identities and social relations.

Consider your own experiences going someplace familiar, like a cafeteria or a church or a faculty meeting. You know what you are getting into and what range of relations and texts and objects and practices will likely be in place and be expected. Your previous experiences with these things lead you to "adopt a frame of mind, set your hopes, plan accordingly, and begin acting with that orientation" (Bazerman, 2002, p. 14). We might consider, then, the ways a text, an activity, or a situation—likely familiar and recurrent in some way even while it is also altogether new—teaches and conditions people to take up, or as Charles Bazerman puts it, to be "caught up" in a particular way.

Take an example from the Community Literacy Center in Pittsburgh in which a youth and his teacher were worlds apart in the ways they constructed a "writer." Raymond and other local teens were working on a publication about drugs that would primarily be written for other teens, from a teen's perspective. They worked hard to combine straight talk from a range of perspectives, to include pros and cons, and to create a text teens would read. Raymond's own ambitious plan included a play script, a flashback, and a dialogue with a reader. Two weeks away from publication, Raymond's mentor at the Center was called to jury duty and then Raymond landed a welcome but unexpected summer job that took Raymond away from the project. However, rather than pulling out of the project or simplifying his task, Raymond chose to work at the Center on his own after his job to finish the text. His other commitments kept him from attending the final editing session, but his final document was impressive despite its rough edges. Proud of his work, Raymond included a picture of himself with the byline: "Raymond Musgrove, Playwrite" (Flower, 2008, p. 189).

The teens leveraged their texts to facilitate a community problem-solving conversation. Many community members and teachers attended, including Raymond's English teacher. Many teachers were shocked and delighted to see these composed, expressive, published *writers* standing up, initiating a dialogue with adults, their peers, and the neighborhood. For many teachers, this event revealed youth capacities they had not seen in their classrooms. This event also marked a turning point for many of them as teachers envisioned possibilities for these young people as rhetorical agents, local knowledge experts, and decision-makers in ways they had not previously imagined (Flower, 2008, p. 192).

However, leveraging their writing in purposeful and public ways, these youth positioned themselves as something other than, something more than "basic writers"—a move toward establishing an identity not everyone would grant. Shortly after the community conversation, word got back to the CLC mentors that Raymond's English teacher was angry. As Linda Flower (2008) recounted, "His unedited text, with its mix of unconventional punctuation and dialogue, Black English Vernacular, and garden-variety errors of grammar and spelling was proof enough of her contention: we had puffed him up. It seems he now thought he was a "writer." And this made her job—of showing him that he indeed was not—twice as difficult" (p. 189).

Raymond's English teacher and the activities of his English class cued him to see himself as not-a-writer, much in the same way that some tests will position some writers nearly all of the time as "basic writers" (Dryer, 2008). This experience is not merely a school-based phenomenon. All of us are at some time positioned as "basic writers." Think about some of your own experiences—perhaps filling out tax returns or reading insurance documents or trying to change zoning ordinances—in which you've encountered forms and activities that seem simultaneously to be in place for you to take some action and yet, in place in such a way as to confuse or limit the action you might most need to take. The forms instead let you know "the way things are" and what is and is not possible for you. In those instances, you are constituted through "the bodily experience of frustration and feeling thwarted by a document's opacity, feeling one's 'place' as an inexpert and therefore excluded reader" (Dryer, 2008, p. 516). You are required to transact with inaccessible texts and people, both clearly signaling a system you must be part of but one that is unresponsive to you, impossible for you to change.

And yet these systems and our ways of being in these systems are changeable. After all, under other conditions and with different cues, Raymond came to experience himself as a writer, despite being constituted at school as not-a-writer. In another high school across town, Sam is seen as an activist and called on as a mentor for teachers caring for transgender youth even though his own school requires him to sit in the front office any time gendered practices or activities—during Valentine's week, homecoming week, sex education, prom week, and the like—occur in school.

If identity construction is, in part, about what any of us do with the multiple x-marks we inherit, then classrooms that support dialogical selves might take up tensions over x-marks, over conventions—gendered pronouns associated with particular genitalia, dress codes, which Englishes are sanctioned, protocol with police or other authority figures—as a site of inquiry not only about what is but, more importantly, about what could be, and especially about *who* could be.

The perpetuation of established conventions constitutes again and again particular kinds of people, particular identities, within networks of social relations that forestall change and limit ways of being to a circumscribed set of options. Focusing on the construction of identities requires a resistant pedagogy of conventions, one that does not oppose learning current conventions. Instead, it takes up the more difficult task of resisting and working against dominant ideologies embedded in contemporary conventions, and doing this in a way that leads to transformation of self, of others, and of conventions (Chase, 1988).

Merely teaching conventions—of language, of dress, of behavior—is not enough to foster ideological becoming because that simply asks students to engage in a certain set of conventions without knowing how those conventions work to reproduce the status quo and to limit the possibilities of their own identities. Instead, we would do well to engage young people in what Bourdieu (2000) calls "practical comprehension" as well as "intellectual comprehension." Bourdieu distinguished the intellectual comprehension we tend to think of as an "intentional act of conscious decoding" (p. 135) from practical comprehension, or "unknow[ing] confusedly what depends on me and what does not, what is 'for me' or 'not for me' or 'not for people like me,' what is 'reasonable' for me to do, to hope for, and to ask for" (p. 130).

Moving Forward

As teachers of reading and writing, we must teach the intellectual comprehension of texts and conventions. And yet our instruction—if we are to cultivate more expansive possibilities for *being, doing,* and *becoming*—cannot stop there. We must also consider young people's experiences with those conventions, especially those conventions where they most experience learning which identities and ways of being are "not for people like me." A resistant pedagogy that takes up practical comprehension might make the constraints of conventions a point of departure for inquiry and discussion.

For example, classmates engaged in a resistant pedagogy start by learning more about their experiences of current conventions. Extending Dylan Dryer's (2008) work considering a resistant pedagogy heuristic in relation to city zoning ordinances, we offer, as a launching point for your own heuristics, some questions young people might ask each other in relation to conventions of dress codes, homecoming week, classroom decorum, testing, adult interactions, writing in and out of school, and so on.

- "Where do you feel most constrained?"
- "What, specifically, are the conventions that you find most frustrating? What is frustrating to you about those conventions?"
- "Why might those conventions work the way they do? How do you account for the ways those conventions typically function?"
- "What kinds of readings or writings or actions are more or less possible with conventions like these?"
- "What might the ways you feel positioned by this text or this convention say about the power relations it reflects and projects?"

Importantly, a resistant pedagogy would also consider changing conventions that are harmful and would especially consider the ways conventions work to keep people from changing them. After considering common conventions, young people might ask:

- "Who gets to revise these conventions, and how is that done?"
- "What happens to those who try to revise these conventions?"
- "What do these conventions teach other than what they say they are intended to teach? What do these conventions do other than what they are intended to do?"
- "What are some other possible conventions? What possibilities do those other conventions allow that these conventions do not?"

In a resistant pedagogy, a student's outsider perspective is a chief advantage in that they can see and begin to articulate some of the values inherent in conventions that others might simply take for granted. A resistant pedagogy, thus, considers not only the construction of an individual's own identities but also the social construction of others' identities, and raises the means of reproduction as a primary site of ongoing deliberation.

Of course, conventions are necessary for efficient, and sometimes effective, communication, and Lisa Delpit (2008) might tell us that attending to the role of conventions is a necessary part of literacy instruction. But a stance toward conventions of "You know, that's just the way it is! You have to learn to play the game guys! I'm sorry," like the prevalent one linguist Samy Alim (2004) documents in an interview with a teacher, aims at what is already constructed as possible. Delpit, too, might argue that learning conventions without learning how to critique, unpack, and trouble conventions is its own kind of marginalization.

These approaches to conventions—either one that completely ignores them or one that suggests students blindly accept them—are not equipped to challenge or expand the scope of what seems possible. A pedagogy that fosters dialogical selves and ideological becoming must then counterbalance "the way things are" with "the way things could be." However, this is not mere escape; nor is it naïve. Just as the "*real*" is sometimes valued as a corrective to the *ideal*, in the same way, considering the "*ought to be*" (Branch, 2007; Horton, 1961) is a necessary corrective to the *status quo*. Resistant readings of the conventions of identity construction are, therefore, a praxis of grounded hope— both a way of looking outside the limitations of the possible to ask how what is currently possible came to seem like the only things that are possible and as a way of imagining more just possibilities for ourselves and others.

References

Alcoff, L., and Mohanty, S. (2006). *Identity politics reconsidered*. London: Palgrave Macmillan.

Alim, S. (2004). Hearing what's not said and missing what is: Black language in white public space. In S. Kiesling and C. B. Paulston (Eds.) *Intercultural discourse communication* (pp. 180–197). Hooken, NJ: Wiley-Blackwell.

Bakhtin, M. (1981). *The dialogic imagination: Four essays by M. M. Bakhtin*. C. Emerson and M. Holquist, Trans. Austin, TX: U of Texas Press. (Original work published 1975.)

Barton, D., and Hamilton, M. (1998). *Local literacies: Reading and writing in one community*. New York: Routledge.

Bazerman, C. (1994). Systems of genres and the enactment of social intentions. In A. Freedman and P. Medway (Eds.) *Genre and the new rhetoric* (pp. 79–101). Bristol, PA: Taylor & Francis.

Bazerman, C. (2002). Genre and identity: Citizenship in the age of the internet and the age of global capitalism. In Coe, et al. (Eds.) *The rhetoric and ideology of genre: Strategies for stability and change* (pp. 13–37). New York: Hampton Press.

Bourdieu, P. (2000). *Pascalian meditations*. Richard Nice, Trans. Stanford, CA: Stanford UP.

Branch, K. (2007). *Eyes on the ought to be: What we teach when we teach about literacy*. Cresskill: Hampton Press.

Butler, J. (1993). *Bodies that matter: On the discursive limits of sex*. New York: Routledge.

Camus, A. (1996). *The first man*. New York: Vintage Books.

Chase, G. (1988). Accommodation, resistance, and the politics of student writing. *College Composition and Communication* 39, 13–22.

Cisneros, S. (1991). *Woman hollering creek: And other stories*. New York: Vintage Books.

Collins, J., and Blot, R. K. (2003). *Literacy and literacies: Texts, power, and identity*. Cambridge: Cambridge UP.

Delpit, L. (2008). *Other people's children: Cultural conflict in the classroom.* New York: W. W. Norton and Company.

Dhaliwal, A. (1996). Can the subaltern vote? Radical democracy, discourses of representation and rights, and questions of race. In D. Trend (Ed.) *Radical democracy: Identity, citenzship, and the state* (pp. 42–61). New York: Routledge.

Dryer, D. (2008). Taking up space: On genre systems as geographies of the possible. *Journal of Advanced Composition* 28(3/4), 503–534.

Eagleton, T. (2007). *The meaning of a life: A very short introduction.* Oxford: Oxford UP.

Fecho, B. (2011). *Teaching for the students: Habits of heart, mind, and practice in the engaged classroom.* New York: Teachers College Press.

Flower, L. (2008). *Community literacy and the rhetoric of public engagement.* Southern Illinois University Press.

Freire, P. (1970). *Pedagogy of the oppressed.* Myra Bergman Ramos, Trans. New York: Continuum Publishing Company.

Gee, J. P. (2003). *What video games have to teach us about learning and literacy.* New York: St. Martin's Press.

Gee, J. P. (2005). Good video games and good learning. *Phi Kappa Phi Forum* 85(2), 33–37.

Gordon, L. (2000). *Existentia Africana: Understanding Africana existential thought.* New York: Routledge.

Grealy, L. (2003). *Autobiography of a face.* New York: Houghton Mifflin.

Greene, M. (2001). *Variations on a blue guitar. The Lincoln Center lectures on aesthetic education.* New York: Teachers College Press.

Hacking, I. (2007). Kinds of people: Moving targets. *British Academy Lecture* 11 April 2006.

Happe, L. (2013). The body of race: Toward a rhetorical understanding of racial ideology. *Quarterly Journal of Speech* 99(2), 131–155.

Hermans, H., and Hermans-Konopka, A. (2010). *Dialogical self theory: Positioning and counter-positioning in a globalizing society.* Cambridge: Cambridge UP.

hooks, b. (1990). *Yearning: Race, gender, and cultural politics.* Cambridge, MA: South End Press.

Horton, M. (1961). Myles Horton's talk at Experimental Citizenship School workshop, February 19–21, 1961. *Highlander Archives*, Box 40, Folder 4.

Kamler, B. (2001). *Relocating the personal: A critical writing pedagogy.* New York: SUNY Press.

Konnikova, M. (2015, Dec. 5). Born to be conned. *The New York Times.* Retrieved from http://www.nytimes.com/2015/12/06/opinion/sunday/born-to-be-conned.html

Laird, J., DeBell, M., and Chapman, C. (2006). *Dropout rates in the United States: 2004* (NCES 2007-024). National Center for Education Statistics, Institute of Education Sciences, U. S. Department of Education. Washington, DC.

Lyons, S. (2010). *X-marks: Native signatures of assent* Minneapolis: U of Minnesota Press.

Lyons, S. (2012, July 16). Real Indians don't care about Tonto. *Native Appropriations.* Retrieved from http://nativeappropriations.com/category/scott-richard-lyons

Lysaker, J. T. (2006). Young children's readings of wordless picture books: What's self got to do with it? *Journal of Early Childhood Literacy* 6(1), 33–55.

Olson, K., Eaton, A., and Key, N. (2015). Gender cognition in transgender children. *Psychological Science* 26, 467–474.

Proulx, T., and Heine, S. J. (2009). Connections from Kafka: Exposure to meaning threats improves implicit learning of an artificial grammar. *Psychological Science* 20(9), 1125–1131.

Salih, S. (2002). On Judith Butler and performativity. In K. E. Lovaas and M. M. Jenkins (Eds.) *Sexualities and communication in everyday life* (pp. 55–68). New York: SAGE.

Scribner, S., and Cole, M. (1981). *The psychology of literacy.* Cambridge: Harvard UP.

Smith, M., and Wilhelm, J. (2002). *Reading don't fix no Chevy's: Literacy in the lives of young men*. Portsmouth, NH: Heinemann.

Steensma, T. D, McGuire, J. K, Kreukels, B. P. C., et al. (2013). Factors associated with desistence and persistence of childhood gender dysphoria: a quantitative follow-up study. *Journal of the American Academy of Child and Adolescent Psychiatry* 52(6), 582–590.

Tannehill, B. (2014). Do your homework, Dr. Ablow. *Huffpost Queer Voices*. Retrieved from http://www.huffingtonpost.com/brynn-tannehill/how-much-evidence-does-it_b_4616722.html

Yancey, K. B. (1999). Looking back as we look forward: Historicizing writing assessment. *College Composition and Communication* 50, 483–503.

5

AGENCY, IDENTITIES, LITERACIES, LEARNING, CULTURES, AND THE DIALOGICAL SELF

Remember Raymond? Here is a young man working two jobs, attending school, and participating in a summer program with other teens to address concerns they have about their peers and their neighborhood. Now think about his English teacher. It's easy enough to think about her critique of Raymond's writing—and her denial of his own assertion of being a writer—as a denial of his agency, as a refusal to recognize his capabilities, abilities, and informed purposeful choices.

Another reading of her critique might be one of nurturing Raymond's agency. Certainly Raymond's innovative uses of narrative and flashbacks worked powerfully in the setting of the learning center's community conversation, but at school and in other settings, his very same choices might not be viewed as favorably or yield the same results and could, quite possibly, hinder Raymond from achieving his goals. It's not a stretch to think that if his writing does not change over time—if he doesn't do more to have his writing reflect and embrace an understanding of standard edited English—Raymond's English teacher won't be the only one who renames him as not-a-writer.

What options are available, then, to acknowledge the ways institutions and cultural and economic systems unevenly bear down on people while also affirming people's abilities, capacities, and purposeful choices—without defaulting to oversimplified narratives of rugged individualism or cynical narratives of victimhood? What are the kinds of stances and actions we need to be attuned to seeing and valuing and enacting? As teachers invested in the lives of young people, how might we go about doing the caring, patiently precise work of drawing out, giving visibility and presence to a young person's agency—in their own eyes and in the eyes of others? What's more, how would seeing ourselves and others as dialogical selves complicate and invigorate the ways we think about, exercise, and nurture agency?

To cultivate agency in a dialogical self is also to cultivate awareness of selves in dialogue, in flux, and in progress. Holland, Lachicotte, Skinner, and Cain (1998) argued that people's "capacity for self-objectification—and, through objectification, self-direction—plays into both their domination by social relations of power and their possibilities for (partial) liberation from these forces" (p. 5, parentheses in the original). In other words, that which holds us down can also lift us up. This idea is not unlike the concept of a meta-position on the self (Hermans & Hermans-Konopka, 2010), the ability people possess to exit a certain I-position or positions and observe from the outside, so to speak, as an act of self-reflection. And, if you'll grant us one further association, this reflective stance connects to Paulo Freire's (1970) concept of *praxis*, the idea that there is no action without thought and no thought without action.

As Raymond comes to be aware of himself as someone who is leveraging texts for his own purposes, he experiences himself as someone who is a deliberate decision-maker and a writer. For Raymond, awareness came through *doing*; writing in ways that he saw contributing to the shared promise of his neighborhood allowed him to see himself as someone *being* and *becoming* a writer. While Raymond dubbed himself a "playwrite" for the script he'd written to foster community conversations, Raymond never vocalized aspirations for being a playwright beyond the project he'd set for himself at the Community Literacy Center. On the other hand, he did want to be a young man who could navigate Northside at a time when the neighborhood was fraught with social and economic difficulties that had the potential to derail a young person's possibilities for thriving. And he saw that his writing—being a "playwrite"—could be useful in the larger personal and social project he cared about.

As Raymond exercises his own self-determination in thinking of himself as a writer and in doing the hard work of writing for his own purposes, Raymond's teacher seems to experience her sense of agency being curtailed. This is an important tension to mark because it represents a pervasive approach to agency, in which one person's agency necessarily negates another person's agency. And yet, this need not be the case. It is true that recognizing and cultivating our own and others' self-determination might also introduce constraints and limitations. However, to cultivate agency in a dialogical self is to nurture self-determination across I-positions *and* to foster internal and external dialogues that take up the difficulties and hopeful possibilities that emerge as mutually self-determined people engage as equals with one another.

Rather than experiencing a loss of agency, Raymond's teacher instead might have recognized this encounter as a moment of wobble and asked herself, "What would it mean to revise my version of 'writer' to take Raymond's sense of being a writer into account?" It is a powerful act of agency to convert something we experience as a limitation or frustration or loss or uncertainty into an open question, an opportunity, a possibility.

So that's what we examine as we write our way through this last chapter—the possibilities presented to us as teachers and learners through agency. Any question of what agency is or how it works is best understood, and perhaps only really matters, in local instantiations of dialogic action, at once purposeful and constrained. And any discussion of what counts as human agency is really about considering options any of us have for seeing ourselves and others, and for pursuing purposeful ends when faced with conditions and constraints we cannot control in a world not of our making.

What may have become evident as you've read through these pages is that it's really very difficult, most likely impossible, to talk about any of the concepts we've keyed for a certain chapter without discussing the others. To an extent, we've been discussing the concept of agency all through this text. And, although we've devoted a full chapter to a focus on identity, we're not done exploring the implications of constructing identity through dialogue with multiple cultures. As Holland et al. (1998) reminded us, constructions of identities are "the key means through which people care about and care for what is going on around them" (p. 5). It's that idea of *caring through identity*, of seeing the ways we position self and other, that has powerful implications for how we act in, respond to, enter into, avoid, entertain, participate in, seek to change cultural contexts. It's that intersection of identities and agency that we unpack in this chapter.

Unpacking Agency

Popular notions of agency in movies and novels and comic books point to heroes and heroines who, against all odds, somehow manage to exert their will on the world, often to bring about some change. And while there may be something comforting about the idea or the hope that any of us can bring about what is most needed simply by wanting it or working hard, that is not, by and large, how most of us experience or enact agency. Certainly, American mythos of rugged individualism and a bootstraps work ethic promote a kind of muscled-up sense of agency that will not be thwarted, but most of us brush up against the limits and outer edges of this version of agency on a regular basis, and it doesn't take that much—an email, a pink slip, a re-Tweeted photo, a mandatory curriculum map, a flat tire, a lost phone, a tornado, student loan debt, an unexpected illness—to remind us just how much willful action is constrained. Agency is, then, "a paradox. We have it and we do not have it. Some of us have it more than others, but no one has it absolutely or lacks it absolutely" (Joseph, 2006, p. 238).

Just this short popular description of some of the myths and conundrums of agency raises some questions about a person's ability to act meaningfully: Where does power ultimately reside? Are human beings free to make rational, intentional, willful decisions, or are their actions ultimately enabled and constrained, at least to some degree, by social, political, and economic structuring structures? (Bourdieu, 1968).

Human agency—something we'll distinguish later from nonhuman agency of technologies, texts, and so on—is often associated with an individual's or a community's assertion of will, and yet agency "is about more than voluntary control over behavior" (Lantolf & Thorne, 2016, p. 143). Agency also includes the "ability to assign relevance and significance to things and events." The relevance or significance any of us assign, the behavior options we recognize as available to us, and the structuring structures that bear down on us are historically and culturally situated. Human agency is, then, historically and culturally situated; it is socially embedded. The options—ways of using language, character traits, particular activities, pathways—open to a person are contextually enacted ways of being in the world, ways that are more open to some than others, and ways that might not have been open as agentive choices at all 20 years ago.

Like identity, agency is thoroughly social (Desjarlais, 1997, p. 24). Holland et al.'s (1998) notion of "history in person" is useful here. As Holland and her coauthors (1998) pointed out, our seeming ability to act independently, as individuals, is possible because the "intimate terrain" of our lives is an "outcome of living in, through, and around cultural forms practiced in social life" (p. 8). This history in person, "the sediment from past experiences", enables one to act in agentive ways. We would add that these *histories*—plural—in person, converging, diverging, *dialoguing,* provide the material "upon which one improvises, using the cultural resources available" (p. 18). Holland et al. recognize that the implication is, of course, a radical claim about human agency: that there is no such thing as an individual act or an individual choice. Instead, all our agentive acts are woven into the social fabric of past, present, and future responses.

This notion may sit uneasily with some of you. However, an individualistic approach to agency oversimplifies the complex social relations, the processes of history and culture, the multiple I-positions, and the ongoing internal and external dialogues in which and through which identities and agency develop. Instead, with regard to agency, we might consider "who has and lacks it in what contexts" (Joseph, 2006, p. 239), a position echoing Desjarlais's (1997) call to consider "the means of action specific to a person, a group, an institution, or a social setting" and to consider how "these ways of acting differ from person to person, place to place, and time to time" (p. 201).

Expanding Understandings of Agency

Even while agency is often deemed a human activity, interactions with recent technologies are changing the ways we think and talk about agency. In scientific writing and in some other kinds of academic writing, agentive properties are assigned to *something* besides the human researcher: "The research study contends that …" or "The hurricane destroyed the beach." Think back to the school signs we described in Chapter 3. Perhaps students and teachers ignore those signs. We could just as easily say that those signs ignore students, and yet they command attention and incorporate students and teachers into a particular kind of social arrangement.

Take a different example, like Coca-Cola slogans on a teenager's shirt in New Delhi or "respectable elderly women" on a Polynesian atoll wearing Western style tee shirts with risqué slogans in English, gifts from family members who work away from the island (Besnier, 1995, p. 71). Like the signs in the school hallway, even when people ignore the texts, the texts act on people, in this case incorporating people into Western consumer culture. Even when a person does not specifically invite or sanction a particular text, a text has incredible agentive capacities including "a capacity to travel, a capacity to stay intact, and a capacity to be visible and animate" outside immediate interactions (Brandt & Clinton, 2002, p. 344). Brandt and Clinton note that it is important to recognize that things, including texts, "are not just acted through or upon by readers and writers" (p. 348). Objects themselves have agency serving as "comrades, colleagues, partners, accomplices, or associates in the weaving of social life" (Latour, 1996).

Tee shirts on bodies, signs in hallways and classrooms, cell phones in pockets are not merely background. Instead, they construct and constrain a social sphere themselves, "endowing meaning to the locales in which they appear" (Brandt & Clinton, 2002, p. 348). Just as objects have agentive properties, so too are spaces and contexts agentive in that they organize patterns of activity, of using language, of relating. They *do something* to people—they *act on* people—by legitimizing some acts but not others, by assigning different values and functions to people's cultural and linguistic repertoires, by constraining some people's options differently in those spaces, and by limiting what a person thinks is not only sanctioned but possible. And things like signs and spaces act on a person whether or not someone else is present.

Of course, the mediating effects of a space are constructed by people as they engage in the social practices that constitute a particular space. That is, space is "always *someone's* space … filled with norms, expectations, conceptions of what counts as proper and normal" (Blommaert, 2010, p. 6, italics added). Space constrains people's interactions, even as people decide what to do with those constraints. However, people's interactions are not simply located in a place; they also *produce* that place as well as the people in it (Pennycook, 2010). In this way, a space or context is not a backdrop or a context for people's interactions but an "interactive and mediating element" (Pennycook, 2010, p. 140).

To think about spaces, like classrooms; or machines, like drones; or technologies, like smart phones; or texts, like curriculum maps or standardized tests, to think about all these entities having agency requires a rethinking of conventional notions of agency that have centered on intent, which has typically only been assigned to conscious, rational human beings aware of their own motivations. This conventional conception of agency conflates motivations with long-term goals and with affective, psychological, or ideological forces that drive individual decision-making. This conception also limits and places agency solely within the mind of a person. Rather than recognizing agency as an *a priori* mental capacity of living or nonliving entities, we see agency as mediated. Agency unfolds and is enacted in activity with others. This view of agency focuses on possibilities, which can be altered by mediation of an artifact: it is possible for people to act in ways that without that object or text or space or technology would not be possible.

The converse is also true. For example, Blommaert, Creve, and Willaert (2006) observe that many immigrants who move to relatively homogeneous, heavily monolingual contexts tend to be automatically associated with language problems and are often rendered "language-less and illiterate" because they do not speak the local (standard) language even though they are fully expert in several languages (p. 53). A multilingual speaker's *linguistic* agency—something we'll later distinguish from other kinds of agency—shifts in terms of the language possibilities expected and in terms of the ways others perceive a person's linguistic capabilities from one space to another. A person's capacities may not have changed from one space to another, but a person's agentive possibilities may have. Space, thus, is neither neutral nor empty.

To illustrate this point, consider a Korean Ph.D. student studying in the United States. Depending on her experience and level of fluency with English, she might feel more hesitant to assert her views in the classroom. There, among students who grew up speaking the language, she possibly would often defer to others, particularly if she were the only Asian present. However, if she and some of those students left class and hopped into a cab driven by a Korean migrant, her ability to converse in Korean might impel her to take the lead in explaining the group's destination. Furthermore, if some of those students were to visit her after graduation at her new teaching position in Seoul, they might discover that the quiet and demure young woman they remembered from class was seen by her colleagues as a leader and by her students as an authority. Although other cultural factors would be in play in these scenarios, certainly the spaces that the student occupied contributed to her differing perceptions of herself and her sense of personal agency.

Enacting Agency

What does all this mean, then, about the ways people enact agency or reclaim agency? Philosopher and ethicist Charles Taylor (1985) placed agency in a world of intractable material conditions. The situations we've already described, and many others that you've experienced in your own life, do not easily bend to the will of a hero, who may him- or herself be far from a free agent. After all, each of us is subject to the natural world, to physical and perspectival limitations, and to the unquestioned assumptions of his or her culture. Even so, each of us, must decide what to do—what and who we will be and become—over and over again, in different situations, where our options are uniquely and familiarly constrained. What a person does with situational constraints and affordances, historically and culturally produced, is at the heart of human agency.

Taylor argued that agency is the act of taking an action, even when few actions are available to us, based on a vocabulary of worth or value. Taylor's value-based choice is different than intent or motivation. It is instead contextually evaluative—determining and, at times, inventing possibilities; assigning those options different, perhaps conflicted, values; and choosing an option to exercise here and now, even if refusal and mute testimony seem to be the only tools and even if the choice does little to alter external circumstances. The poet June Jordan's students performed this version of agency when they chose to write a letter to the editor in all caps Black English, knowing that it likely would not be published and that it could not change the fact of Willie Jordan's death. Still, the choice to assert their language, their solidarity, their Blackness in a world that would kill it, was a powerful declaration of worth, a powerful act of agency.

Similar agentive choices can be seen in acts of silence or refusal. Consider an instance when Eileen, a Navajo student in an American history class, "critically used silence to shield [her] identities, [her] stories, [her] realities" (San Pedro, 2015, p. 134). After a year of choosing to actively not learn the materials presented in her American history class because of the ways the instructor and her classmates denied and denigrated Native American people and histories, Eileen found herself again sitting in the same American history course with the same teacher, hoping this time around might be different. And yet it wasn't.

One day in particular, Eileen asked her teacher to discuss Chief Sitting Bull, an important historical figure. The instructor did not know who Chief Sitting Bull was and instead made a joke: "Sitting Bull? As in Cheech and Chong?" Eileen sat in shock while her classmates laughed. San Pedro stories Eileen's experience this way:

> I was just so shocked.
> The class laughed and I was
> sitting there
> with this really disgusted look on my face
> because they were being disrespectful,
> and I was really pissed.
> I was like,
> > "How the hell does this American history
> > teacher not know who he is?"
> …I was so shocked by that whole concept of it.

(p. 147)

As the teacher and students ridiculed Eileen for knowing an American historical figure, they pushed Eileen's knowledge to the periphery. The space of the classroom, for Eileen, took on an agency of its own, one of erasure, that resulted in her "just sitting there with this really disgusted look on her face … in silence" (San Pedro, p. 148). Of course, this interaction and others like it were painful for Eileen. In this moment, she exercised her agency by speaking up. In that interaction, her silence may have marked confusion, frustration, anger, and astonishment in addition to the disgust and shock she names. However, over time, she weighs other options and learns "*not* to verbalize her truths, her realities, or her emotions" (San Pedro, p. 148). Instead, she chooses silence. Through her silence, she exercises an agency of resistance to Eurocentric teachings and ways of being with those in the room, and she exercises an agency of protection for her self, her culture, her beliefs.

Sometimes a person has time to reflect and engage in self-deliberation to determine the most desirable act of agency, even among limited choices, but often a person must determine possibilities, evaluate them, and enact one (or more) in a flash as an interaction unfolds in real time. Importantly, even when there is little time to assess options in the moment, agentive acts also produce objects of reflection, of possible ongoing dialogue and evaluation. This is important for a person making sense of her own behavior and constructing her agency going forward and for understanding and constructing the perceived agency of others.

Agency is constructed in the dialogical space between *first-person information*, the way an individual experiences his or her own activity, and *third-person information*, the way a person experiences someone else when observing him or her in an activity (Barresi, 2002). When any of us engage in social action, we take into consideration our own understanding of our self and put that information in conversation with the ways we think someone else—perhaps a principal or a parent—might imagine us. Alongside that dynamic, we also include what we imagine the other person thinks of himself plus what we directly experience of that other person. While this may seem like a lot for a person to process, remember that this is also occurring among and across multiple I-positions. The negotiations of this multiplicity in human and post-human interaction—all of the ways we see possible for ourselves to show up *in dialogue with* the multiple ways we expect, anticipate, grant, and limit others showing up *in dialogue with* the contexts we move in, out of, and among—shape the very conditions of agency. Together, in this highly complex dialogue, we make sense of our own agentive capacities and constraints in relation to the agentive options of others (Hermans & Hermans Konopka, 2012, p. 179).

Agency in Schools

Take this extended interaction in a Michigan high school (Kirkland, 2013). A teacher walks down the hallway, her presence scattering fistfight participants and spectators. As she approaches, she sees a journal on the floor that belongs to Derrick, a student of hers who had been watching the fight. Flipping through the journal, she sees symbols, drawings, handwritten rhymes and, impressed, wonders, "Why doesn't he write like this in class?" Her question reflected a larger conversation going on at her school around literacy and Black males. Kirkland noted that "many at the school described quite a few of their Black male students as struggling readers and writers—what the school described as a 'crisis' for which it seemed to have no solution. As a consequence, some of the other teachers in the school complained, 'The [Black] boys won't read or write anything'" (p. 18).

A couple of days later, the teacher approaches Derrick and returns his journal, admitting that she read some of it. She apologizes and tells him, "You are a writer, Derrick. I don't see any of this out of you in the class. You and your friends, Shawn and the gang, just sit in the back of the classroom and stare. You're not doing great in my class, and it's not because you can't do the work. That book in your back pocket says that you can. I just want to understand how I can help" (Kirkland, p. 19).

In her comment the teacher acknowledges the promise and capabilities demonstrated in Derrick's journal. She directly perceives him as a writer just as she directly perceives Derrick and his friends staring in the back of the room. To make sense of what she perceives, she also must imagine Derrick and his friends. She does not seem to imagine that there might be any value to writing powerfully in his personal notebook and yet choosing not to write in the ways that she and school requires. She acknowledges a *capacity for* agency but does not recognize his literacy practices for his own purposes as a powerful act *of agency*. Her question tries to neatly package his agency, to point it in a direction, to leverage it toward the ends she would have him choose. Seeing that he could participate in school-based practices and yet chooses not to, she *imagines* Derrick and "position[s] him in her comment not only as helpless, but also as powerless—as wasted potential" (Kirkland, p. 19).

Derrick, however, experiences himself and his teacher quite differently. For Derrick, his literate practices were "more complex than his experiences with books [and classrooms] could reveal" (Kirkland, p. 4) and "intimately connected to [his] stories" (p. xiv). His notebook was filled with creative language that wrestled with complex issues most pressing to him, "places no one goes in school" (p. 138). Derrick had little use for the work of school that was so far removed from his own life and his own powerful ways of using language. Neither was he willing to participate in the "narrative of pity that plays leitmotif in the lives of too many people of color" (p. 120). So Derrick smiled at his teacher and responded, "Miss, thank you, but I don't need your help."

While the teacher is in some ways well-intentioned but misguided, she attempts to open up a dialogical space with Derrick. What is important to mark here is how central ways of imagining the self and others is to the construction of agency—our own and others'. The teacher's way of imagining Derrick limits not only Derrick's agentive choices but also the teacher's. Part of the reason she talks to Derrick about his notebook is because she is uncertain about what to do and feels like she might "have missed the boat somewhere" (Kirkland, p. 19). Until the teacher reads the notebook, a questionable action to be sure, she does not seem to be aware of Derrick's capabilities. And yet, being introduced to another way of seeing Derrick—Derrick as *writer*—does not automatically foster new agentive possibilities for either Derrick or the teacher. This is, in part, because each of our histories-in-person run deep, producing and limiting what we even imagine to be possible for ourselves and others.

Earlier in the chapter we noted that identity construction is closely linked to how we "care about and care for" the cultural contexts we engage (Holland et al., 1998). Ian Altman, a high school teacher in Georgia who we mentioned in Chapter 1, exemplifies this process well. As an undergraduate philosophy major, Ian admittedly came to teaching English through a less traditional path, which may account for his readiness to imagine multiple ways of engaging students in the study of literature and composition. As someone who thinks deeply and critically about the texts and contexts of his life, he expects the White, Black, Latino/a, and Asian students that populate his classes to do the same. Whether the children of professors or the children of workers in a chicken processing plant, Ian urges students to unpack what they read, see, experience, and hear in ways that reveal the complexity beneath the surface idea.

It was not a surprise then, when various governing bodies began to pass laws and policies limiting the rights of many of his Latino/a students, that Ian would see himself calling such actions into question and pushing back against them. These were students who had come to the United States as young children, who had been chiefly educated in US schools, and who were achieving academically. Yet, the state of Georgia had barred what they termed "undocumented" students from applying to the five major state-run universities and relegated such students to paying out-of-state tuition if they were accepted at the remaining state schools. In effect, policymakers had erected a huge wall at the border between high school and college intended to effectively keep these students from furthering their education and adding to the quality of life in Georgia.

As a way of bringing multiple perspectives and silenced voices to the dialogue, Ian and a colleague, along with support from University of Georgia faculty, pulled together a forum in which several un(der)documented students were able to share their concerns, their aspirations, and their stories with an audience of educators and the general public. Ian has written (Altman, 2016) about how the composing of these talks, as opposed to so much of school writing, was generated from an ongoing dialogue among his students, their experiences, their concerns, their contexts, and his gently probing questions. Rather than merely complying with a class assignment, the students embraced the personal stake they had in this writing and engaged the work as a meaning-making activity for them and others. They had volunteered into this public forum and cared about what they would say, how they would say it, and what the opportunity to have their voices at least recognized and heard might mean for furthering recognition of their issues.

As a result of this dialogical process, the students had crafted highly personal, yet deeply political talks. How, they wondered, could a person be deemed illegal, as if their very existence was somehow against the law? If they had committed themselves to the promise of education, why was that promise feeling so empty when it should have been a rich handful? What was to be learned when a nation of immigrants once again denied the newest immigrants the opportunities of others?

What was to be gained by limiting bright young minds from full engagement in the democratic process?

Ian also wrote about the risks of agency—of his students "outing" their lack of sufficient documentation, at least as that lack was viewed in the eyes of authorities; of his own risk of being seen as someone involved in a protest that many in Georgia disagreed with, of the complexity of taking a public position on a political issue, yet allowing his students to come to their own understandings on such issues. Sadly, but not surprisingly, Ian was the subject of hate letters calling for his dismissal and worse. Both university and school district personnel were chastised for using state-owned computers and email addresses for political purposes, as if government officials didn't do that daily and as if anything in education could be deemed nonpolitical. Perhaps most distressingly, a state legislator who attended the forum confronted one of Ian's students, and tried to bully her into admitting to being a criminal. As Ian noted with pride, the student held her ground until he intervened.

Ian would be the last person to describe himself as a hero, and that's not the point of sharing this anecdote. Instead our intent is to point out that our capacity for agentive action frequently comes to a matter of choice, even among limited and confusing choices. Ian could have decided that this was not his battle to fight, that it was best professionally to not be overtly political, or that he would work quietly behind the scenes. Moving in other directions, Ian could have organized a walkout at his school, chained himself to the bumper of a state legislator's car, or resigned his position in protest, being unwilling to support such policies by his continued presence in the system. We are in no way arguing that any of these options—and scads more than what we could list here, but at the risk of boring you—is in some way the better, the more correct, the preferred or right one. Instead, as we've argued throughout the book in terms of meaning making, cultural transactions, learning, and identity construction, we respond in context, and context almost always presents us with complexity.

Part of this complexity resides in the several I-positions that contexts can call into play. Looking again at this example, Ian-the-teacher felt it important to support students he taught, students he saw not as "illegals" or "criminals" or as "undocumented", but as adolescents seeking an education. Ian-the-husband-and-father worried about putting his job on the line and thus placing the economic security of his family in jeopardy. Ian-the-professional was careful not to make his cause that of his students, nor to insist they agree with his position. That same I-position may have wondered if the students of other races and ethnicities, his colleagues, and the administration respected or decried his strong support of his Latino/a students. Ian-the-philosophy-student continued to run logical arguments about the implications of these policies, and Ian-the-activist sought to devise ongoing means to raise the issues for and the consciousness of the general public.

Undoubtedly, such contexts come with unifying/controlling and individualizing/destabilizing tensions. An almost elephant-in-the-room tension is one regarding that which is legal and that which is ethical. The laws and policies of Georgia were in the authoritative voice we wrote of earlier in the book (Bakhtin, 1981). Nothing less than absolute and unquestioned compliance was expected. Yet, Ian and his students felt an ethical need to call such policy into question. Then there is what might be construed as a zigzag of conflicting tensions from educational stakeholders: the Board of Regents wanting X, state legislators wanting Y; administration perhaps tugged between supporting teachers and students and seeing that central administration and Department of Education policy is carried out; some parents wanting a teacher who just taught—whatever that means—and others joining Ian and his students in their efforts. And certainly tensions existed between the mainstream culture of schools that tends to portray a cohesive surface calm and the needs of students who are relegated to the margins due to that pretension of unity and serenity.

We would like to report happy endings, but complexity rarely yields such ever afters. As of this writing, the policies limiting un(der)documented students matriculating at state universities in Georgia remain intact and in force. A conservative legislature seems intent on finding more ways to further limit these students and their families. Happily, Ian still teaches and the efforts of a committed group of educators have formed an organization, U-Lead, that supports un(der) documented students in their quest for equity in higher education. Work done by U-Lead has led to students finding scholarships, loans, and other means of aid to attend mostly private institutions outside Georgia. But organizations like U-Lead come into being because caring individuals operationalize whatever degrees of agency they can in the cultural contexts they encounter.

POST-DIALOGICAL

Framing the Dialogue (Jen)

Even though this is a book about selves in dialogue and about navigating through dialogue to gain direction, the nature of our own dialogue and of our selves-in-dialogue regularly surprised us throughout our writing together. This final sidebar narrates personal arcs of our joint sense making.

Jen's Take

Throughout our writing together, each of us has taken turns at initiating chapters or lines of thought and at responding to those initiated by the other. I regularly found myself both astounded and in love with Bob's prose and thinking and alternately pausing and feeling tensions as it seemed clear that we each had different priorities and disciplinary concerns. Bob leans toward prizing individual agency while I lean more toward exposing the ways systems constrain agency, and constrain some people's agency in concentrated, patterned, and disproportionate ways. I tend to align myself more with marginalized young people while Bob aligns more with caring and conscientious teachers. Bob thinks of dialogue more cerebrally in relation to meaning making while I think of dialogue more in relation to the gritty pragmatics of complex problem solving across differences. These aren't either/or positions, of course; we move back and forth among these and others, but these particular leanings really matter for us and for the people we most have in mind when we do this work.

As far as writing together, I found myself at times—in light of our differences—initiating and responding from a stance that was to some degree protective. I didn't want our theorizing to miss or minimize the principles and scholarship and people I care most about. After several middle chapters of this productive tension, I felt uncertain heading into the final chapter. I had no idea what would feel like closure for the book and with Bob.

When Bob sent me the pages he ventured toward the end of the final chapter to pull together our shared ideas across the book, I was floored. That I was floored gives you some idea about the very real tensions I experienced as we wrote—even in the face of deep solidarity and shared commitments with Bob. As I read, I found myself softening, opening up, delighting, and also in some way feeling relieved. I sensed the need I'd felt to be protective dissipating. I was reminded why we wanted to write together and think together all along—something I'd experienced throughout our time together, but something that also at this moment felt in some ways more restful and sweet.

All this to say, that writing the final chapter, and especially reading/hearing what Bob was making of our work together was, at least temporarily, *post*-dialogical. There was a sense of remembering *and* a very real way in which we had arrived in an altogether new space together. And somehow, our tensions over negotiated meanings and our practices for constructing something shared while allowing for dissensus had been productive. And somehow, what was shared and what is now newly shared was and is *more rich* precisely *because of* the multiple dialogues and multiple I-positions—and the centripetal and centrifugal pull—we each contributed. It is the very process of *doing* and *being* and *becoming* together that made this text rich and sweet for us, and we hope, for you.

Bob's Take

When I reflect on this working relationship—one that is still being tested and one that actually does work—I realize that I was writing with a stranger. Before Jen sent me that email that introduced her to me, I had no idea that she existed on the planet. Since then, we have met in the same physical space no more than three times, and although we have Skyped more often than met face-to-face, those e-meetings can probably be counted on one hand. Yet, even from the first tentative ideas that we blogged, I could feel in Jen's words such deep conviction to ideas, to causes, to people, and for the first time in a while, writing for me became mostly about learning, about seeing in new ways, about taking chances. Although I believe that writing is almost always a meaning-making activity, sometimes it is more than others and in Jen's swirling, dynamic sentence structure and fierce allegiances, I found myself making links in ways that surprised me in how much absolute sense they made and wondering why hadn't I drawn these links earlier.

Jen writes of tension, and it existed for both of us. I remember an email I sent indicating how much I worried when I forwarded new sections of a chapter draft to her. One would think that as the senior member of this partnership that wouldn't be the case for me. But I was, in this text, pushing myself where I urge so many teachers to go, to slip in to that space where my gathered understandings were put into motion, were, in fact, wobbling. I was forcing myself to construct more nuanced understandings as I was co-writing with someone who seemed intimately steeped in many of the thoughts I was just exploring. And I was crossing cultural boundaries, while trusting someone who I barely knew to give me the space to, at times, cross those boundaries less gracefully than I might have wanted.

Which is why I sent ahead what amounts to the final section of our last chapter. It needed to resonate with ideas and thoughts that neither of us alone could have written—at least not in their present context—without the writing dialogue that we had both engaged in. Where we came out needed to be threaded back to where we entered, but needed to show new colors, shades, variations, deepenings, engagements, directions, and tones. It needed to vibrate across the distance between New York and El Paso. It needed, to paraphrase Bakhtin, to taste of both of us as individuals and as a collective. And, as Jen wrote above, it is the very process of *doing* and *being* and *becoming* together that made this text rich and sweet for us, and we hope, for you.

Takeaways

Really, we can't give you any. If you have any smidgeon of belief in transactional or reader response theory, then you'll grasp that no matter what we try to do as writers, you'll take from our writing that which you'll deem most furthers your ongoing dialogue about these issues. You'll, in fact, create a text that is not the text we wrote, but the one you interpreted. Your text will in many ways resemble our work as we imagined it, but it will only contain in bold font that which we didn't necessarily intend to bold, those ideas that confirm, question, expand, engage, complicate, nuance, clarify, and/or trouble your worldview. This is your agency.

For our part, no matter how dialogically we tried to work, that "work as we imagined it"—the text that each of us thinks we wrote—is somewhat different for both of us. Bob's text and Jen's text frequently dovetail, but often take individual flights of thought, singular shifts of tack. Parts of what we wrote matter more to one of us than it does to the other, although the entire text matters deeply to both of us. We invested much more than time in this work; we've invested our multiple selves as well. That is our agency.

Yet we spent over two years in dialogue with some common intentions, ideas that we see as important and that we argue need to enter the ongoing dialogue about cultures, learning, literacy, identity and agency and how they transact in our lives. In particular, we've introduced the theory behind the dialogical self that, heretofore, has mostly been part of the educational dialogue outside the US, and even there not in any mainstream context. We brought this roiling mix of ideas to your attention because, as people with a stake in education, you will need to contend with the ways cultures play out in schools and we think that you and future students will be ill-served if teachers and administrators and policymakers continue to view cultures in simplistic and monolithic ways.

The Importance of Context

If you reflect over what you've just read, you'll quickly realize that one significant thread that weaves through this book has been our discussion of the fluidity, the complexity, and the omnipresence of context. Meaning is made in context. Cultures transact in context. Learning occurs in context. Literacy practices are engaged in context. Identities are in process in context. Agency occurs in context. All of the above are affected by the sway and pull of context. We live our lives in response to context. In doing so, we continually shape who we are becoming and we shape the contexts we are responding to.

Doing the exact same thing or saying the exact same words within different contexts will always yield variations on the interpretation of what has occurred and what needs to occur next. Saying, "Hey you bastard" to a good friend might get you a warm bear hug in return; saying the same thing to a taxi driver who just picked you up at the corner will no doubt yield less pleasant results. This concept helps to explain why "best practices" aren't. Because classrooms occupy different spatial, temporal, and cultural contexts, what takes place and seems to operate well in one classroom cannot be dropped wholly into another classroom with the expectations of the same results. Which is not to say that such practices can't be *adapted*, but such adapting needs to be done in reflective and thoughtful ways that are ever mindful of the shift in and shifting contexts. We act, learn, interpret, devise, construct, and remain in context.

The Importance of Complexity

And those contexts are complex, particularly for those of us who routinely transact globally through technology. Complexity does not favor simple solutions, and rarely favors any solutions at all. Instead, complexity yields changed contexts when we respond within it. Often changes that occur may be, at least for the time being, for the better, but usually such changes may reveal hidden relationships that are problematic or conjure new relationships that create heretofore unthought of issues. A case in point: antibiotics that are used to combat deadly bacteria have raised rates of longevity and decreased deaths among children, but the prevalence and misuse of antibiotics have also provided fertile ground for antibiotic-resistant bacteria to thrive. When Sir Alexander Fleming was growing the first penicillin cultures, he most likely didn't imagine all the changes in the complex contexts that might occur. He was intent on saving lives. Still, his efforts changed the contexts of all our lives, with subsequent and often unforeseen benefits and issues.

Despite efforts by many policymakers to view teaching and learning in simplistic or, at best, complicated ways, what happens in classrooms most often occurs within a complex context. Consider the classroom choice of moving student desks into a circle. It's seems a relatively benign move. Hopefully, such a change would cause your understanding of how you teach to wobble as you consider what such a change means for the work you do with students. You've shifted the context in ways that allow for more eye contact among all in class and should facilitate more verbal engagement because students can't hide behind others. Something about a circle makes everyone feel included, as well. However, students sometimes feel more exposed and thus vulnerable in a circle. If you have to accommodate 25 or more students, the circle's diameter is so large the face-to-face intimacy you hoped for gets lost. Then there's those times when you want students quiet and focused—silent sustained reading for example—but having eye contact with everyone in the room prompts transactions, which is often why you put students into a circle in the first place.

All you did was move some furniture, but you did it in the complexity of a living classroom. Rather than having you throw up your hands in exasperation at this complexity, we ask you, instead, to attune to it, be cognizant of it, make it part of the ways you and your students negotiate learning. Look at your classroom, make note of what's happening there, think reflectively about it, and then make decisions based on that process. However, don't expect solutions. Instead start the process again to help you better understand what seems to be positive within this changing context and what remains or has become problematic.

The Multiplicity of Cultures

One component of the complexity that is a classroom is the multiplicity of cultures that dialogue there. Although a course may be offered to sophomores at a girls high school catering only to upper middle class Whites—hopefully such a school no longer exists—the teacher facilitating that course would be off base to think that she teaches in a monocultural context. Physical capacities, religious backgrounds, spirituality, family composition, gender identity, sexual preference, political camps, social media engagement, food choice lifestyles, leisure time engagements, and many, many other social factors create a significant multicultural mix in the room. No educator teaches within a monocultural context, even if tutoring only one student.

Teachers approaching such situations—that is to say all teachers—should enter from an inquiry-based, dialogical stance. The idea is not to be an expert on all the cultures that transact in your classroom. Even attempting such would be impossible. Instead, the idea is to be sensitive to this range of cultural opportunity in order to inquire into and dialogue with it. To acknowledge that this complex range of cultures exists and to act on that knowledge is to see all students for the unique individuals they are without disregarding the many cultural positions and contexts they bring with them. It allows you to be open to a moment when, say, a Black adolescent male reading James Baldwin responds more deeply to the author's homosexuality than his Blackness.

The Internal and External Dialogue

The young Baldwin student we just described was responding from an I-the-gay-male position more so than an I-the-Black-male position, although there's no denying that both I-positions were in dialogue as he read the text. We've cited many examples throughout the book in which our many I-positions are in dialogue with each other and with external contexts. The idea of multiplicity within unity has driven much of how we've examined, discussed, reflected on, and argued about cultures and identities. We wrote it much earlier in the book, but it bears repeating: humans are multicultural beings dialoguing with multicultural contexts.

It also strikes us that the concept of multiplicity within unity becomes a useful metaphor for so many of the contexts we engage daily. A family—no matter how it's composed—represents multiplicity within unity. So does a classroom, a school, a bowling team, a street gang, a neighborhood, a gaming site, a city, and so on. When we join that bowling team we simultaneously become part of the culture of bowling enthusiasts and of the specific culture of that team. Both cultures shape us, but so, too, do we shape those cultures. And although others on your team would miss their child's high school graduation if it clashed with the championship tournament, your I-as-father position might argue differently.

Wobble and the Possibilities of Uncertainty

Trying to decide if you should, for the sake of the team, miss your child's graduation is a wobble moment, a point in time when you're compelled to pay attention.

Such moments call into question our positions, our identities, our beliefs. When they occur, multiple voices engage. I-the-teammate doesn't want to let the team down, while I-the-parent doesn't want to let your child down. Maybe I-the-child remembers a time when one of your parents or an adult caregiver missed an important event in your life or I-the-achiever really covets winning that championship. External voices join in. Your significant other doesn't understand why you're even vacillating, while the team captain pleads several times for your presence at the tournament. Your child has become moody and silent about the whole business.

A wobble moment generally places us in a context of complexity and one of uncertainty. There is no clear path to take necessarily, no one right decision that becomes a win for all stakeholders. Through dialogue, however, some possible directions in which to move start to clarify. You begin to consider what takes priority in your life, what values you value more, what implications this response will have on future response. Although such situations are never easy, through dialogue you develop the nuances within your belief system, the nuances that help you to better understand your actions and the actions of others. That which may have caused initial dread develops into a context rife with possibility. As a teacher, such moments encourage you to keep your practice in process.

The Constant Process of Being, Doing, and Becoming

As we've illustrated many times along the way, your teaching practice isn't the only part of your life in process. Our lives are on an ongoing process of being, doing, and becoming. A teacher in a university course once worried about where to draw the line when encouraging students to question their beliefs. "I don't want to change their minds," she exclaimed. Yet how can we who teach not change their minds? That's really the core of what teachers do. In education, we change minds. It's what parents who adhere to fundamentalist values fear most about public school—that it will change their children. And they are right. Education is about change. It is not a system of verification or confirmation. It is not a system of inheritance. Nor is it a system of replication. Education is about change—of minds, perspectives, values, understandings, meanings, selves—really all the tools through which we construct cultures and identity.

Paulo Freire (1970) wrote that humans know they are incomplete and because we know that, we continue to learn. We can't help but change. Education is never neutral. Learning is never in a vacuum. Instead we learn in contexts shaded by our experiences; peopled by our many cultural selves; inhabited by friends, families, mentors, enemies, and a literal cast of millions.

Consider the consequences if we don't see our lives and identities as a constant process of being, doing, and becoming. Are people all that they will ever be at birth, either chemically or divinely programmed to act or respond in predefined ways? Do we as humans resemble an onion; peel away enough layers and you'll discover an inert core? Is life about seeking, finding, discovering, revealing an essential you, something that remains completely untouched and unchanged by the many cultural transactions you've encountered and will continue to engage? Why do we learn if all there is to learn is already there, or has already been thought by others and now is yours not to explore but to swallow whole?

Learning from Many Positions

We aren't much for the idea of swallowing learning whole. Follow that metaphor far enough and you'll understand what happens to most learning done that way. We instead see learning as a generative act facilitated by the multiple I-positions all learners bring into play. As you've been reading this text, we have no doubt that more than one of your I-positions has been brought to bear on the ideas we've been presenting. If no others, I-the-learner and I-the-teacher have dialogued with the text and with each other. Others may have also engaged: I-the-skeptic? I-the-believer? I-the-parent? I-the-child? I-the-writer? I-the-gatekeeper? I-the-conservative? I-the-liberal? Still others, we're sure, could be identified.

It is these multiplicities of positions, at least in part, that help individuals and cultures remain dialogically in process. Without the flux and flex provided by dialogues across the many positions people encounter internally and externally, it is difficult to imagine any opportunities for new ideas, discoveries, relationships, or learning in its myriad of forms. As historian David Christian (2011) related in his TED talk on what he calls Big History, it is the human capacity to chronicle, share, and build from our collective history that allows and will allow us to negotiate the increased complexity of our lives and our knowledge constructions of the universe we inhabit. When we bring many positions to the table of complex issues we increase our possibilities for taking future directions that will have more positive and fewer negative repercussions. This point applies to individuals seeking insight into who they are becoming and cultures seeking to do the same just on a larger scale.

Constructing Cultures through Participation

When people participate in a culture, at least two actions occur: individuals construct themselves in relation to the culture and cultures construct themselves in relation to individuals. Of the two constructions, the former is more evident to people as they go about their daily business. Someone starts yoga classes and begins to pursue a more healthful lifestyle or attends a new church on a whim and starts constructing a more religious sense of self. As individuals, we are well aware of the ways we overtly and tacitly transact with a range of obvious and less obvious external cultures.

What is more difficult to see are signs of how, across time, cultures shift in relation to the thoughts, actions, and evolving beliefs and customs of the individuals who participate in them. Most likely the many forms of mass communication—cultures unto themselves even as they spread other cultures—are and will continue speeding up the process of cultural change. Still, in relation to individual identity construction, cultural identity construction is, not surprisingly, more complex and less easily discerned across short time periods. Yet cultures remain responsive to the individuals who participate in those cultures. Changing views on same sex marriage, women's role in society, and the medical use of marijuana are but three indications of cultural shifts that have changed dramatically—although perhaps still not dramatically enough—over the last half century. We have no doubt that there will be many more cultural shifts in the near and distant years to come; however, we can only imagine what those shifts might be and what they will mean to all who participate within those cultures.

Last Words, at Least for Now

When you picked up this book, when you purchased it, when you decided to read it rather than lay it on a shelf, you were taking agentive steps in terms of your learning. You were also being, doing, and becoming. Whether originally impelled by an instructor as an assignment for course credit or initiated by you in an attempt to widen and deepen your grasp of multicultural issues, your transactions with this book positioned you within several cultural contexts to which you responded. It simultaneously triggered dialogue across a number of internal I-positions. Perhaps you wrote in response to some of the issues presented, engaged in book circle discussions gathering differing perspectives, or drew connections from arguments we made in the text to other texts, other experiences. Maybe you took the time to consider how some of your beliefs had been called in question, paused as you felt yourself ever so slightly wobble, and then moved dialogically into that context of uncertainty.

Having written this book, our contexts, our identities, our avenues of agency, our constructions of cultures are all in flux. We have raised issues with each other, shared favored resources, fretted over language choice, and developed sometimes paralleling, sometimes dovetailing, sometimes differing narratives. We have deleted, copied, pasted, cut, and commented on the digital page and in that part of our brains that remained focused on this text even when we weren't at the keyboard. Having written, we are different.

We suspect, having read, you are different as well. As we have dialogued with each other in the writing, we have invited you into the dialogue. We wonder what you're thinking, are curious about how you've responded and how you will continue to respond, want to know where—if anywhere—you became more aware of the self you had constructed to date and the self you continued to construct. We hope that some part of your mind—really some significant part of your self—long after you've shelved this text, keeps in dialogue with these ideas, continues to construct and give voice to multiple I-positions, remains willing to engage multiple perspectives in the classroom, and leaves you open to that unsettling, but also enlivening sense of wobble.

References

Altman, I. (2016). Ian's story. In B. Fecho, M. Falter, and X. Hong (Eds.) *Teaching outside the box but inside the standards: Making room for dialogue* (pp. 45–64). New York: Teachers College Press.

Bakhtin, M. (1981). *The dialogic imagination: Four essays by M. M. Bakhtin.* C. Emerson and M. Holquist, Trans. Austin, TX: U of Texas Press. (Original work published 1975.)

Barresi, J. (2002). From 'the thought is the thinker' to 'the voice is the speaker': William James and the dialogical self. *Theory and Psychology* 12, 237–250.

Besnier, N. (1995). *Literacy, emotion, and authority: Reading and writing on a Polynesian atoll.* Cambridge, New York: Cambridge University Press.

Blommaert, J. (2010). *The sociolinguistics of globalization.* Cambridge, New York: Cambridge University Press.

Blommaert, J., Creve, L., and Willaert, E. (2006). On being declared illiterate: Language-ideological disqualification in Dutch classes for immigrants in Belgium. *Language and Communication* 26, 34–54.

Bourdieu, P. (1968) Structuralism and theory of sociological knowledge. *Social Research* 53(Winter), 681–706.

Brandt, D., and Clinton, K. (2002). Limits of the local: Expanding perspectives on literacy as a social practice. *Journal of Literacy Research* 34(3), 337–356.

Christian, D. (2011). David Christian: The history of our world in 18 minutes. [Video file]. Retrieved from https://www.ted.com/talks/david_christian_big_history?language=en

Desjarlais, R. (1997). *Shelter blues: Sanity and selfhood among the homeless.* Philadelphia: U of Pennsylvania Press.

Freire, P. (1970). *Pedagogy of the oppressed.* Myra Bergman Ramos, Trans. New York: Continuum Publishing Company.

Hermans, H., and Hermans-Konopka, A. (2010). *Dialogical self theory: Positioning and counter-positioning in a globalizing society.* Cambridge: Cambridge UP.

Holland, D., Lachicotte, W., Skinner, D., and Cain, C. (1998). *Identity and agency in cultural worlds.* Cambridge, MA: Harvard University Press.

Jordan, J. (1998). Nobody mean more to me than you and the future life of Willie Jordan. *Harvard Educational Review* 58(3), 363–375.

Joseph, J. (2006). Applied linguistics and the choices people make (or do they?). *International Journal of Applied Linguistics* 16(2), 237–241.

Kirkland, D. (2013). *A search past silence: The literacy of young black men.* New York: Teachers College Press.

Lantolf, J. P., and Thorne, S. (2006). *Sociocultural theory and the genesis of second language development.* Oxford: Oxford University Press.

Latour, B. (1996). On interobjectivity. Symposium on "The lessons of simian society." Mind, Culture and Activity (www.ensmp.fr/~latour/Articles/63-interobjectivity.htm).

Pennycook, A. (2010). *Language as local practice.* New York: Taylor & Francis.

San Pedro, T. (2015). Silence as shields: Agency and resistances among students in the urban southwest. *Research in the Teaching of English* 50(2), 138–153.

Taylor, C. (1985). *Philosophical papers: Volume 2, Philosophy and the human sciences.* Cambridge, NY: Cambridge University Press.

ABOUT THE AUTHORS

Bob Fecho is a professor of English Education at Teachers College, Columbia University where his work continues to focus on issues of language, identity, sociocultural perspectives, and dialogical pedagogy as they relate to adolescent literacy among marginalized populations. His single and co-authored books include *Teaching Outside the Box but Inside the Standards: Making Room for Dialogue; Teaching for the Students: Habits of Heart, Mind, and Practice in the Engaged Classroom; Teaching Literature to Adolescents* (3rd edition); and *"Is This English?" Race, Language, and Culture in the Classroom*, the last of which received the James N. Britton Award (CEE/NCTE) recognizing exemplary studies published by English/language arts teachers. His work has also received the Richard Meade Award for Education Research (CEE), as well as the Alan C. Purves Award (NCTE), which honors articles published in *Research in the Teaching of English* most likely to influence classroom practice.

Jennifer Clifton is an assistant professor of English (Rhetoric and Writing Studies) at The University of Texas at El Paso. Her research and teaching brings the situated knowledge of everyday people into intercultural spaces of inquiry and deliberation, not only for dialogue across differences, but for co-constructing wise rhetorical and transformative action within concrete contexts of struggle. Her expertise is in rhetorical education that bridges in- and out-of-school civil and civic literacies and partners with marginalized rhetors to effect social, political and economic change in public spheres. She has a forthcoming book, *Argument as Dialogue Across Difference: Engaging Youth in Public Literacies* (Routledge, 2017). Other select publications include "Writing as Dialogue Across Difference: Inventing Genres to Support Deliberative Democracy" in the *English Journal;* "Embracing a Productive Rhetorical Pragmatism: Teaching Writing as Democratic Deliberation" in *The*

Journal of Teaching Writing and Writing Teacher Education, "Mastery, Failure and Community Outreach as a Stochastic Art: Lessons Learned with the Sudanese Diaspora in Phoenix" in the edited collection *Unsustainable: Owning Our Best, Short-Lived Efforts at Community Writing Work*, and "Accessing Private Knowledge for Public Conversations: Attending to Shared, Yet-to-be-Public Concerns in the Deaf and Hard-of-Hearing DALN Interviews" in *Computers and Composition*.

INDEX